Word in Season Devotional

Fourth Quarter – Fall

Written by: Earl Cooper, Ph. D
www.DiscipleshipMinistries.ca

ὁ λόγοσ ἐν τῷ λαῷ   ὁ λαόσ ἐν τῷ λόγῳ

Published by:
A Word in Season Ministries
1248 Healey Lake Road
Bracebridge, Ontario, Canada

For additional publications see:
www.AWordInSeasonMinistries.com

A note from Earl:

While pastoring in Bracebridge, Ontario the Lord opened the door for me to write a weekly Bible Devotion newspaper column. This provided a wonderful means of sharing God's word in a broad public format. Over the years of these newspaper column submissions I received many notes of appreciation.

Although I was unable to carry on this column after joining ABWE Canada as a travelling teacher, I added a selection of these devotional submissions to my website to offer a full year of daily devotions for the many who continued to request them. The expressed appreciation of the website devotionals led to publication of these as four Daily Devotion Books – Winter, Spring, Summer, Fall.

It has never been my intention to encourage God's people to substitute written Daily Bible Devotions for daily, personal Bible reading and Bible study. I urge each reader to be encouraged by these devotional thoughts personally, and to use these devotions to minister to others by any means appropriate. However, I also urge each reader to go beyond reading Bible devotions written by myself, or any other, and develop the essential Christian disciplines of systematically reading through the entire Bible regularly, daily studying the Bible inductively, and writing your own Bible Devotion Journals of what God has taught you through study. Although the labour is demanding work, the rewards are 'out of this world.'

Be diligent to present yourself approved to God, a worker who does not need to be ashamed, rightly dividing the word of truth. 2 Timothy 2:15
"It is written, 'Man shall not live by bread alone, but by every word that proceeds from the mouth of God.'"
Matthew. 4:4

October 1
Matthew 14: 25-33

Now in the fourth watch of the night Jesus went to them, walking on the sea. And when the disciples saw Him walking on the sea, they were troubled, saying, "It is a ghost!" And they cried out for fear. But immediately Jesus spoke to them, saying, "Be of good cheer! It is I; do not be afraid." And Peter answered Him and said, "Lord, if it is You, command me to come to You on the water." So He said, "Come." And when Peter had come down out of the boat, he walked on the water to go to Jesus. But when he saw that the wind was boisterous, he was afraid; and beginning to sink he cried out, saying, "Lord, save me!" And immediately Jesus stretched out His hand and caught him, and said to him, "O you of little faith, why did you doubt?" And when they got into the boat, the wind ceased. Then those who were in the boat came and worshiped Him, saying, "Truly You are the Son of God."

Safety within Reach

It is always a shock to hear of a family who perish in a house fire when stored away in that house is a fire alarm which could have saved all, if it had been installed. An even greater tragedy occurs daily as countless numbers of people, within reach of eternal life, pass into eternity because they have never appropriated the means of their salvation.

Charles Spurgeon, known as "the prince of preachers" once wrote "It will not save me to know that Christ is a Saviour; but it will save me to trust him to be my Saviour. I shall not be delivered from the wrath to come, by believing that his atonement is sufficient; but I shall be saved by making that atonement my trust, my refuge and my all."

Be reminded of these Bible verses: "If thou shalt confess with thy mouth the Lord Jesus, and shalt believe in thine heart that God raised him from the dead, thou shalt be saved. For with the heart man believeth unto righteousness and with the mouth confession is made unto salvation."(Romans 10:9-10). It has been said of this verse that people can miss heaven by twelve inches, the distance between the mind which knows that safety lies in Christ and the heart which never in faith reaches out to receive Him. The epistle of John emphasises this point of decision: "He came unto his own, and his own received him not. But as many as received him, them gave he power to become the sons of God, [even] to them that believe on his name" (John 1:11-12).

The Bible clearly states that faith in Christ alone secures salvation: "For whosoever shall call upon the name of the Lord shall be saved" (Romans 10:13). This is a faith that turns the heart in sorrow from sin (repentance) to Christ's substitutional death (belief). Scriptures are clear when they state "For by grace are ye saved through faith; and that not of yourselves: [it is] the gift of God: Not of works, lest any man should boast". (Ephesians 2:8-9). Therefore, the securing of salvation is not dependent upon any works of man such as being baptized or joining a church. These follow the point of decision.

It is not the lifebuoy on board the ship that saves a drowning man, nor his belief that it can save him. No, he must take hold of it or else he will sink. Don't perish with the multitudes in reach of safety ... accept God's free gift of life through faith in Christ today. "For God so loved the world ,that he gave his only begotten Son, that whosoever believeth in him should not perish, but have everlasting life." (John 3:16).

Personal Notes:

October 2

1-6

LORD? Will You forget me forever? How long will [hide You]r face from me? How long shall I take counsel in my soul, Having sorrow in my heart daily? How long will my enemy be exalted over me?
Consider and hear me, O LORD my God; Enlighten my eyes, Lest I sleep the sleep of death; Lest my enemy say, "I have prevailed against him"; Lest those who trouble me rejoice when I am moved. But I have trusted in Your mercy; My heart shall rejoice in Your salvation. I will sing to the LORD, Because He has dealt bountifully with me.

Dealing with Anxiety

Few would deny that human life is swayed by care. This is by no means considered inappropriate for most realize that all people have some measure of responsibility. The ordinary cares concerning food, clothing, and housing, have in recent past been taken for granted in this country. However, such is not the case for many today. These essential cares have become a point of anxiety as the means of supply has slipped from grasp. In such difficult times few need to be reminded that anxiety tears away at the very fibre of life leaving despondency, depression and despair, which seem insurmountable.

The Bible gives a simple, yet meaningful, answer to those who are anxious: "Be careful (anxious) for nothing; but in everything by prayer and supplication with thanksgiving let your requests be made known unto God. And the peace of God, which passes all understanding, shall keep your hearts and minds through Christ Jesus" (Philippians 4:6-7).

The Christians at Philippi were under duress through economic and political circumstances. To them, Paul gave this answer for an anxious heart; "pray with thankfulness". On first glance this undoubtedly seems too simple, yet Paul reminded the Philippians of two meaningful facts: they belonged to God, "our citizenship is in heaven" (Philippians 3:20), and Christ as Lord of all had the power "to bring everything under His control" (Philippians 3:21, NIV). The answer for a troubled heart was rooted in faith in God's commitment to His children's best interests (as special citizens) and God's ability to meet every need (through unlimited power). Sharing the requests in prayer acknowledged God's care, thanksgiving reflected the faith in His answer as being completely appropriate. The result was a promised peace of mind.

This same peace can be found today by following the Philippians' example of accepting the gospel message (Philippians 1:5), believing that Jesus paid the penalty of sin in his death then rose from the dead (1 Corinthians 15:3-4) and humbly surrendering their lives to God's will and care. This privileges the believer with the opportunity to express the requests on our hearts and trust God for what is best, understanding these circumstances as a means of developing a deepening dependence upon God.

A peace that passes human understanding even in the most anxious of times can be found through prayer that springs from a relationship with God through the gospel, and a trust upon God that can be thankful in all things.

Personal Notes:

October 3
Isaiah 11: 15-12:3

The LORD will utterly destroy the tongue of the Sea of Egypt; With His mighty wind He will shake His fist over the River, and strike it in the seven streams, and make men cross over dry-shod. There will be a highway for the remnant of His people who will be left from Assyria, as it was for Israel in the day that he came up from the land of Egypt.
And in that day you will say: "O LORD, I will praise You; Though You were angry with me, Your anger is turned away, and You comfort me. Behold, God is my salvation, I will trust and not be afraid; 'For YAH, the LORD, is my strength and song; He also has become my salvation.'" Therefore with joy you will draw water from the wells of salvation.

The Anchor Holds

Several years ago a family crossing Lake Erie in their newly purchased sail boat narrowly escaped loss of life. As they travelled from Cleveland toward Port Burwell, a storm developed which began to toss their boat around mercilessly. To avert destruction the novice sailors cast their anchor out from the stern. The waves crashed over the stern, tearing the anchor loose and capsizing the boat. Fortunately, although the boat was destroyed, the family was washed ashore in safety, wearing life jackets.

This story reminds me of the words of an old hymn: "Will your anchor hold in the storms of life?" God speaks of an anchor that all men need: "Because God wanted to make the unchanging nature of his purpose very clear to the heirs of what was promised, he confirmed it with an oath. God did this so that, by two unchangeable things in which it is impossible for God to lie, we who have fled to take hold of the hope offered to us may be greatly encouraged. We have this hope as an anchor for the soul, firm and secure. It enters the inner sanctuary behind the curtain" (Hebrews 6:17-19 NIV). Here God makes a promise and an oath to confirm the hope of salvation as an anchor of the soul.

See first the description of this anchor. It is "sure", meaning safe or unbreakable. Like the four inch steel cables that secure the anchors of great ships, this hope of salvation is an unbreakable anchor. It is also "steadfast", meaning solid, grounded and unmoving. This hope of salvation cannot shift; time and circumstance will not shake or move it.

See next the location of this anchor. It is within "the inner sanctuary". This is the place of the very presence of God "where Jesus, who went before us, has entered on our behalf." (Hebrews 6:20 NIV). Our hope of salvation is an anchor as sure and steadfast as the power of God in raising Christ from the dead. Our anchor is the Lord Jesus Christ, who "died for our sins according to the Scriptures, ... was buried, (and) ... was raised on the third day according to the Scriptures, (1 Corinthians 15:3-4 NIV).

As the storms of life come, many seek refuge in financial security, inner strength, or even "religion" (without a personal relationship with God). Often too late, these people find their error; the anchors do not hold! There is only one sure anchor of deliverance in our present circumstances and for eternity- Jesus Christ the Son of God. To know him is to be assured of safe arrival (like wearing life jackets), but to follow Him (hold to His Word as authority and guide in life - "Thy word [is] a lamp unto my feet, and a light unto my path." Psalms 119:105) is to be held secure through storms by the anchor of hope. What is your anchor of security?

Personal Notes:

October 4
Romans 5: 15-21

But the free gift is not like the offense. For if by the one man's offense many died, much more the grace of God and the gift by the grace of the one Man, Jesus Christ, abounded to many. And the gift is not like that which came through the one who sinned. For the judgment which came from one offense resulted in condemnation, but the free gift which came from many offenses resulted in justification. For if by the one man's offense death reigned through the one, much more those who receive abundance of grace and of the gift of righteousness will reign in life through the One, Jesus Christ.) Therefore, as through one man's offense judgment came to all men, resulting in condemnation, even so through one Man's righteous act the free gift came to all men, resulting in justification of life. For as by one man's disobedience many were made sinners, so also by one Man's obedience many will be made righteous. Moreover the law entered that the offense might abound. But where sin abounded, grace abounded much more, so that as sin reigned in death, even so grace might reign through righteousness to eternal life through Jesus Christ our Lord.

Amazing Grace

Weakness is looked down upon today with such vigour that few would even admit any element of personal weakness. This was not the case with the apostle Paul. He was inflicted with an ailment which he believed to be a detriment to his ministry. Three times he pleaded with God to heal him, however God had another plan. The Lord chose to leave Paul with the struggle in order to privilege him with experiencing the sufficiency of God: "he (God) said to me, "My grace is sufficient for you, for my power is made perfect in weakness." (2 Corinthians 12:9 NIV). Paul found a depth of strength in the GRACE of God, a resource worthy of consideration in these troubled days.

Like a rainbow with many colours, grace has a broad spectrum of meaning, each nuance rich with blessing. Grace is first that which affords joy or delight because of intrinsic beauty. The Lord said in essence "the beauty of My Person is sufficient for you." As the Lily of the Valley and The Bright and Morning Star, God's very beauty brings joy and strength to those who know Him.

Grace is loving kindness, good will, and special care. Jesus demonstrated this in His continual care for the sick and the suffering as he reached out to touch the needy. Essentially, God said "My loving care is sufficient to you". All who have taken hold of eternal life through the loving sacrifice of Christ on the cross know the meaning of this love.

Grace is the ordering of circumstance to guarantee good to the benefactor. It is the special attention of God toward those whom He holds dear as "the apple of His eye". To Paul, God said "My special favour toward you is sufficient". A quick review of Paul's escapes from shipwreck, peril, and evil plots confirm his declaration: "we know that in all things God works for the good of those who love him, who have been called according to his purpose." (Romans 8:28 NIV) Those who follow the Lord realize that there are no coincidences. The hand of God moves to guarantee the believer's good and God's glory.

Grace is a gift, the bestowal of ability. God said "My enabling is sufficient for you". God graced Paul's life with the ability to complete his ministry. As well, grace is the expression of appreciation. God declared "My reward is sufficient for you". With Paul, every Christian should understand the sufficiency of the means of service - God's equipping, and motive for service - His reward.

Is it any wonder that, having experienced the deep and abiding sufficiency of the GRACE of God, Paul declared with conviction and anticipation: "Therefore I will boast all the more gladly about my weaknesses, so that Christ's power may rest on me ... For when I am weak, then I am strong." (2 Corinthians 12 NIV). The GRACE of God affords strength to His people in direct proportion to their own weakness in order for God to receive all the Glory. Dear Christian friend, isn't it great to be weak?

Personal Notes:

October 5
Genesis 1:26-31

Then God said, "Let Us make man in Our image, according to Our likeness; let them have dominion over the fish of the sea, over the birds of the air, and over the cattle, over all the earth and over every creeping thing that creeps on the earth." So God created man in His own image; in the image of God He created him; male and female He created them. Then God blessed them, and God said to them, "Be fruitful and multiply; fill the earth and subdue it; have dominion over the fish of the sea, over the birds of the air, and over every living thing that moves on the earth." And God said, "See, I have given you every herb that yields seed which is on the face of all the earth, and every tree whose fruit yields seed; to you it shall be for food. "Also, to every beast of the earth, to every bird of the air, and to everything that creeps on the earth, in which there is life, I have given every green herb for food"; and it was so. Then God saw everything that He had made, and indeed it was very good. So the evening and the morning were the sixth day.

God Created

"In the beginning God created ... "(Genesis 1:1). These are words that have been barred from many schools and scientific establishments as "purely religious", having no merit in the halls of higher learning. A careful and unbiased look proves otherwise. The word 'created' ("bara" in Hebrew) means to call into existence that which had no existence and is only used in the Bible of the work of God. God alone can create out of nothing "... the universe was formed at God's command, so that what is seen was not made out of what was visible." (Hebrews 11:3 NIV).

Dr. Henry Morris, former chairman of the Civil Engineering Department at Virginia State University, points out the scientific significance of these first words of Genesis 1:1: "the physical universe was spoken into existence by God. It had no existence prior to this primeval creative act of God. God alone is infinite and eternal. He also is omnipotent, so that it was possible for Him to call the universe into being. Although it is impossible for us to comprehend fully this concept of an eternal, transcendent God, the only alternative is the concept of an eternal, self existing universe; and this concept is also incomprehensible. Eternal God or eternal matter - that is the choice. The latter is an impossibility if the present scientific law of cause and effect is valid, since random particles of matter could not by themselves generate a complex, orderly, intelligible universe, not to mention living persons capable of applying intelligence to the understanding of the complex order of the universe. A personal God is the only adequate Cause to produce such effects."

These are not just the thoughts of a solitary engineer and scientist. Darwin himself expressed his own doubts about a creation without a creator. In a letter to Asa Gray, dated April 3, 1860, Darwin wrote: "To suppose that the eye with all its inimitable contrivances for adjusting the focus to different distances, for admitting different amounts of light, and for the correction of spherical and chromatic aberration, could have been formed by natural selection, seems, I freely confess, absurd in the highest possible degree."

Some of the world's greatest scientists, past and present, have understood and accepted the relevance of those five small words, "In the beginning God created ...". Francis Bacon who developed the Scientific Method accepted an original Creation by God as did Isaac Newton who developed the laws of dynamics, gravity and calculus; and Gregor Mendel who founded the modern science of genetics. Indeed, Genesis 1:1 not only belongs in the science class, but many see these words as the very foundation of true science.

The next time you are out admiring the wonders of our beautiful creation, take a moment and consider this: "The heavens declare the glory of God; the skies proclaim the work of his hands." (Psalms 19:1 NIV). If God made all this beauty, could He not also make your life beautiful? "Therefore, if anyone is in Christ, he is a new creation; the old has gone, the new has come!" (2 Corinthians 5:17 NIV).

Personal Notes:

October 6

Psalm 91: 1-11

He who dwells in the secret place of the Most High Shall abide under the shadow of the Almighty. I will say of the LORD, "He is my refuge and my fortress; My God, in Him I will trust." Surely He shall deliver you from the snare of the fowler and from the perilous pestilence. He shall cover you with His feathers, and under His wings you shall take refuge; His truth shall be your shield and buckler. You shall not be afraid of the terror by night, nor of the arrow that flies by day, Nor of the pestilence that walks in darkness, Nor of the destruction that lays waste at noonday. A thousand may fall at your side, and ten thousand at your right hand; but it shall not come near you. Only with your eyes shall you look, and see the reward of the wicked. Because you have made the LORD, who is my refuge, Even the Most High, your dwelling place, No evil shall befall you, Nor shall any plague come near your dwelling; For He shall give His angels charge over you, To keep you in all your ways.

The Snare

The snare, with its alluring bait and suddenness of capture, can result (if not used properly) in slow, merciless death by starvation or strangulation, and therefore, can be one of the craftiest and cruellest, yet most successful forms of hunting. It's no surprise, therefore, to find God's description of Satan's work as 'snares set for men'.

In 2 Timothy, we are told that people are in the snare of the devil when they resist the gospel message which declares we are saved by faith in Christ's death and resurrection alone, rather than good works. "Those who oppose him he must gently instruct, in the hope that God will grant them repentance leading them to a knowledge of the truth, and that they will come to their senses and escape from the trap of the devil, who has taken them captive to do his will" (2 Timothy 2:25-26 NIV).

Satan has deluded these people and trapped them into doing his will. They face an awful and everlasting separation from God as Christ himself declared: "Then they will go away to eternal punishment, but the righteous to eternal life" (Matthew 25:46 NIV).

"Caught in a snare" also describes the danger men incur when they strive for wealth and exclude God: "People who want to get rich fall into temptation and a trap and into many foolish and harmful desires that plunge men into ruin and destruction" (1Timothy 6:9 NIV). Our nation's addiction to lotteries and bent toward gambling will continue to bear witness to this truth, as people who can hardly afford food and clothing pour their money away on such vices.

Another snare is mentioned in I Timothy 3 where, because of inexperience leading to false pride, church leaders become prey for Satan. He captures them in his power and renders them unfit for God's service. The result is shame to Christ and isolation from Christians.

These snares are very real and dangerous; the only hope of escape is found in turning to Christ who by His mercy and grace offers salvation through His own sacrifice. The maintaining of fellowship with God through salvation brings genuine protection: "For he who dwells in the shelter of the Most High will abide in the shadow of the Almighty ... For it is He who delivers you from the snare of the trapper and from the deadly pestilence." (Psalm 91). Why be caught in a deadly snare when God can set us free?

Personal Notes:

October 7
Psalm 107: 1-9

Oh, give thanks to the LORD, for He is good! For His mercy endures forever. Let the redeemed of the LORD say so, Whom He has redeemed from the hand of the enemy, And gathered out of the lands, From the east and from the west, From the north and from the south. They wandered in the wilderness in a desolate way; they found no city to dwell in. Hungry and thirsty, their soul fainted in them. Then they cried out to the LORD in their trouble, And He delivered them out of their distresses. And He led them forth by the right way, that they might go to a city for a dwelling place. Oh, that men would give thanks to the LORD for His goodness, and for His wonderful works to the children of men! For He satisfies the longing soul, and fills the hungry soul with goodness.

The Heart of Thanksgiving

There is an old Hebrew legend about two brothers who lived on adjoining properties, one married with a family and one single: One night the married brother said: "God has blessed me with a good wife, strong children, a bountiful harvest and many hands to reap it, but my brother is all alone with no help with his harvest. Let us go to our fields, tie as many bundles of grain together as we can carry and set it on my brother's land to encourage him. At the same time the single brother said to himself, God has blessed me with a bountiful harvest and only my own needs to care for; my brother has many children to feed, I will go this night and bundle as much grain as I can carry and place it on my brother's property to encourage him. And so, in the middle of the night with arms full of grain, the brothers met at the border of their properties. Each recognized the intention of the other and with tender compassion, and tear-filled eyes, they dropped their bundles and embraced, being filled with gratitude. The legend states that the point of the brothers' embrace became the location of the Temple of God.

Thanksgiving, true gratefulness before God, provides a completely different perspective on the world than what others might expect. Yet how little mankind gives thought to "every good gift and every perfect gift that comes from above" (James 1:17), and how little man is moved to practical gratefulness. We have so much of God's blessing, yet are unwilling to give recognition, let alone love and homage to God in faith and obedience.

I'm reminded of the rich young ruler who came to Jesus to find eternal life and turned away from Christ's call: "go, sell your possessions and give to the poor, and you will have treasure in heaven. Then come, follow me." When the young man heard this, he went away sad, because he had great wealth." (Matthew 19 NIV).

No matter how rich this ruler was, he could not go pick up his phone and call a friend, he could not turn on his radio and hear the latest news and weather, he could not escape the heat by eating ice cream or sitting in air conditioned comfort, and he most assuredly could not spend his weekends travelling hundreds of miles in pursuit of entertainment. Putting things in such perspective certainly seems to lay this man's burden of guilt on our society, richer by comparison yet equally unthankful and self-seeking.

On whatever day of the year you celebrate Thanksgiving, don't make the error of the rich ruler, turn to Christ, embrace Him in faith. Then, being filled with gratitude, hear again these words of the Psalmist: "Oh that [men] would praise the LORD [for] his goodness, and [for] his wonderful works to the children of men! And let them sacrifice the sacrifices of thanksgiving, and declare his works with rejoicing." (Psalm 107).

Personal Notes:

October 8
Genesis 3:1-10

Now the serpent was more cunning than any beast of the field which the LORD God had made. And he said to the woman, "Has God indeed said, 'You shall not eat of every tree of the garden'?" And the woman said to the serpent, "We may eat the fruit of the trees of the garden; "but of the fruit of the tree which is in the midst of the garden, God has said, 'You shall not eat it, nor shall you touch it, lest you die.'" Then the serpent said to the woman, "You will not surely die. "For God knows that in the day you eat of it your eyes will be opened, and you will be like God, knowing good and evil."
So when the woman saw that the tree was good for food, that it was pleasant to the eyes, and a tree desirable to make one wise, she took of its fruit and ate. She also gave to her husband with her, and he ate. Then the eyes of both of them were opened, and they knew that they were naked; and they sewed fig leaves together and made themselves coverings. And they heard the sound of the LORD God walking in the garden in the cool of the day, and Adam and his wife hid themselves from the presence of the LORD God among the trees of the garden. Then the LORD God called to Adam and said to him, "Where are you?" So he said, "I heard Your voice in the garden, and I was afraid because I was naked; and I hid myself."

The Bottomless Pit of Sin

In the midst of the Bible's dark passage of man's fall from original grace comes one of the most serene images of scripture: "Then the man and his wife heard the sound of the LORD God as he was walking in the garden in the cool of the day" (Genesis 3:8). Here is a picture of the Lord God, creator and sustainer of the universe, seeking intimate fellowship with man. Here is a portrait of the loving care and tender compassion of *Elohim* - the all powerful one, as He seeks out man, "the apple of His eye".

That beautiful scene is all too quickly shattered: "and they hid from the LORD God among the trees of the garden" (Genesis 3:8b NIV). Rebellion with its ugly claws tore all serenity away. Consequently, there is a bottomless pit that mankind is in, the bottomless pit of sin. Adam jumped into that pit in his rebellion against God and took all mankind with him. "your iniquities have separated you from your God; your sins have hidden his face from you" (Isaiah 59:2 NIV).

For thousands of years man has continued to fall, each generation commencing its descent where the previous left off. Man is farther away from God than ever before. He is so far away that he has forgotten God exists by inventing religions that are atheistic which, focusing on defying God. Humanity is committing itself to an eternity of suffering in the absence of any blessing or goodness of God: "For although they knew God, they neither glorified him as God nor gave thanks to him... they became fools and exchanged the glory of the immortal God for images made to look like mortal man and birds and animals and reptiles" (Romans 1:21-23 NIV).

Into that bottomless pit leading to eternal horror, an arm reaches out to each person, the arm of God's own righteousness. No matter how far man has fallen, God's arm can reach to restore. This arm is Jesus Christ, God's own Son, who, for the love of man descended into that pit in place of man and came out a victor: "... Jesus our Lord... He was delivered over to death for our sins and was raised to life for our justification" (Romans 4:24-25 NIV).

The day is coming when God will restore that picture, shattered by sin so long ago. John was privileged to tell mankind of it: "And I heard a loud voice from the throne saying, "Now the dwelling of God is with men, and he will live with them. They will be his people, and God himself will be with them and be their God. He will wipe every tear from their eyes. There will be no more death or mourning or crying or pain, for the old order of things has passed away" (Revelation 21 NIV). Those who by faith take hold of God's outstretched arm will be a part of that great day. Will you be in that picture?

Personal Notes:

October 9
Psalm 127:1-5

Unless the LORD builds the house, They labor in vain who build it; Unless the LORD guards the city, The watchman stays awake in vain.
It is vain for you to rise up early, To sit up late, To eat the bread of sorrows; For so He gives His beloved sleep.
Behold, children are a heritage from the LORD, The fruit of the womb is a reward.
Like arrows in the hand of a warrior, So are the children of one's youth.
Happy is the man who has his quiver full of them; They shall not be ashamed, But shall speak with their enemies in the gate.

The Gift of Children

Years ago, before inflation and taxes took all the fun out of the malt shop, a little girl sat at the counter and inquired about the cost of a sundae. When she was told "fifty cents", she opened up her fist and studied the coins in her hand. Then she asked how much a plain dish of ice cream would cost. "Thirty-five cents" snapped the busy waitress. Finally the little girl ordered the plain ice cream and gave the waitress thirty-five cents. Later as the waitress was cleaning the counter, she noticed that the little girl had left a tip in her empty dish, two nickels and five pennies. That waitress has kept those seven coins as a gentle reminder that little people are just as important as big people, especially to themselves. The dignity of humanity reaches across all cultures, all races, all social structures and touches little girls at malt shops as well.

A single child, just like an adult, is special in God's eyes! Jesus brought this reminder to his disciples. They had mistakenly sought to prevent children from approaching him. His response to their actions was pointed and unique: "Jesus said, "Let the little children come to me, and do not hinder them, for the kingdom of heaven belongs to such as these." (Matthew 19:14 NIV). The greatest gift and most valuable inheritance that an adult can leave a child is influence that points them to Christ.

Jesus also gave warning to those who would lead children astray: "But if anyone causes one of these little ones who believe in me to sin, it would be better for him to have a large millstone hung around his neck and to be drowned in the depths of the sea." (Matthew 18:6 NIV). God will hold every parent, every teacher, every adult, accountable for the direction that they lead children in.

One hundred years ago, Pastor D.L. Moody challenged the citizens of Chicago with this very thought: "What would have been Noah's feelings if, when God called him into the ark, his children would not have gone with him? If he had lived such a false life that his children had no faith in his word, he would have said: "There is my poor boy on the mountain. Would to God I had died in his place!" Noah loved his children and they had confidence in him, and found safety. Are your children safe in the ark?" (Are they safe through faith in Christ). God has not changed, nor have children's needs!

A trip to Sick Kids Hospital in Toronto brought to my mind the sober reality of the suffering of children. I was grateful for a facility committed to their care, provided through the sacrificial contributions of concerned people. As adults, we must see the whole person and extend that same concern to the spirit and soul as well. In what direction does your sphere of influence point children?

Gentle Jesus, meek and mild,
Look upon a little child,
Pity my simplicity,
Suffer me to come to thee.
Charles Wesley (1707-1788)

Personal Notes:

October 10

Jeremiah 33:6-11

'Behold, I will bring it health and healing; I will heal them and reveal to them the abundance of peace and truth. 'And I will cause the captives of Judah and the captives of Israel to return, and will rebuild those places as at the first. 'I will cleanse them from all their iniquity by which they have sinned against Me, and I will pardon all their iniquities by which they have sinned and by which they have transgressed against Me. 'Then it shall be to Me a name of joy, a praise, and an honor before all nations of the earth, who shall hear all the good that I do to them; they shall fear and tremble for all the goodness and all the prosperity that I provide for it.'
"Thus says the LORD: 'Again there shall be heard in this place—of which you say, "It is desolate, without man and without beast" —in the cities of Judah, in the streets of Jerusalem that are desolate, without man and without inhabitant and without beast, 'the voice of joy and the voice of gladness, the voice of the bridegroom and the voice of the bride, the voice of those who will say: "Praise the LORD of hosts, For the LORD is good, For His mercy endures forever" —and of those who will bring the sacrifice of praise into the house of the LORD. For I will cause the captives of the land to return as at the first,' says the LORD.

Spelling out Thanksgiving

Thanksgiving is spelled in many ways; some spell it h.o.l.i.d.a.y., others spell it f.a.m.i.l.y., and just about everyone spells it f.o.o.d. Have you ever wondered how God spells thanksgiving? In the book of Psalms there is a clear relationship between thanksgiving ("yada" in Hebrew) and the goodness of God.

In such Psalms as 138, 139, and 140, thanksgiving is the expression of a heart that confesses the care, creation and righteous judgments of God. Here, thanksgiving is spelled r.e.a.l.i.z.a.t.i.o.n. It is a heart of praise to God as a result of realizing He alone is benefactor, defence, and salvation of His people: "I will worship toward thy holy temple, and praise (yada) thy name for thy lovingkindness and for thy truth" (Psalms 138:2)

In Psalm 26 thanksgiving is spelled r.e.n.d.i.t.i.o.n: "That I may publish with the voice of thanksgiving, and tell of all thy wondrous works." (verse 7). Here the voice of man is lifted up to render praise to God. This vocal of thanksgiving is expressed in corporate worship, where people gather to give God thanks (Psalm 122); in personal testimony by individuals (Psalm 109); and in songs of praise (Psalm 108).

Perhaps the most meaningful way of spelling thanksgiving is r-e-c-i-p-r-o-c-a-t-i-o-n (the act of mutual giving and returning): "I will offer to thee the sacrifice of thanksgiving, and will call upon the name of the LORD." (Psalms 116:17). This sacrifice of thanksgiving is a reference to the peace offering meal of Leviticus 7:12, when a family would celebrate together their fellowship with God because of the peace they received through forgiveness.

The Lord God culminated the various sacrifices of the Old Testament which brought temporary peace with the sacrifice of His Son: "God will credit righteousness-- for us who believe in him who raised Jesus our Lord from the dead. He was delivered over to death for our sins and was raised to life for our justification. Therefore, since we have been justified through faith, we have peace with God through our Lord Jesus Christ," (Romans 4:24-5:1 NIV). Paul appeals to believers to live out this peace by reciprocation - rendering to God our lives as a living sacrifice. This reciprocation to God in thanksgiving for His sacrifice is the Christian's reasonable duty (Romans 12:1-2), and the best way to spell thanksgiving.

In 1944 a 15-year old boy in Plelo, France was lined up before a firing squad as punishment to the town for harbouring freedom fighters. A small unit of soldiers led by Bob Hamsley risked their lives to stop the massacre. In 1990, that same youth (now mayor of Plelo) located and returned Hamsley to the very spot of the rescue. There the town expressed thanks in ceremony for deliverance. They realized that it is hard to forget your saviour. Thanksgiving, spelled realization, rendition, and reciprocation is simply not forgetting our Saviour.

Personal Notes:

October 11
1 Peter 2:4-12

Coming to Him as to a living stone, rejected indeed by men, but chosen by God and precious, you also, as living stones, are being built up a spiritual house, a holy priesthood, to offer up spiritual sacrifices acceptable to God through Jesus Christ. Therefore it is also contained in the Scripture, "Behold, I lay in Zion A chief cornerstone, elect, precious, And he who believes on Him will by no means be put to shame." Therefore, to you who believe, He is precious; but to those who are disobedient, "The stone which the builders rejected Has become the chief cornerstone," and "A stone of stumbling And a rock of offense." They stumble, being disobedient to the word, to which they also were appointed. But you are a chosen generation, a royal priesthood, a holy nation, His own special people, that you may proclaim the praises of Him who called you out of darkness into His marvellous light; who once were not a people but are now the people of God, who had not obtained mercy but now have obtained mercy. Beloved, I beg you as sojourners and pilgrims, abstain from fleshly lusts which war against the soul, having your conduct honourable among the Gentiles, that when they speak against you as evildoers, they may, by your good works which they observe, glorify God in the day of visitation.

On Being Special

Shortly after Canada's Ambassador Ken Taylor successfully rescued a number of Americans from the threat of becoming hostages, I was in the United States and was treated royally, - even thanked for Ken Taylor's efforts. Canadians had become "special" people in the eyes of our big neighbour and it felt good. There are cities still in Europe I'm told, that because of the efforts of Canadian soldiers during WWII, Canadians are treated with great welcome and fanfare. To these towns liberated by our soldiers, all Canadians are special people, and it makes us feel good.

When God made man in his image, He put a desire in man corresponding to the relationship between God and man. Part of that desire is "to be special". It is to have a sense of importance, to understand and feel our own unique significance. Experiences that raise our awareness of being special are truly gratifying. However, when those experiences are based upon human relationships, something always happens to burst the bubble, to deflate the balloon and descend man to despair.

Paul, writing to the Roman Christians, speaks of a point of privilege, a sense of being special, that belongs to all who receive by faith the gospel message. Paul reminds these believers that their point of privilege is a mountain that cannot fail, a strong tower that can not be crushed or toppled: "To all (believers) that be in Rome, beloved of God" (Romans 1:7). This point of privilege is specifically defined as being "the beloved of God."

In this privilege lies the high place of God's acceptance of the believer. So complete is the gospel's forgiveness and reconciliation that God sees the believer as His own children, honoured even as Jesus Christ the eternal Son. In this lies the honour of God's attention toward each believer whereby He lavishes His gifts and attention and works out His eternal purposes. Peter states this special status of God's people in other terms: "But you [are] a chosen generation, a royal priesthood, an holy nation, a peculiar people; that ye should show forth the praises of him who has called you out of darkness into his marvellous light" (1 Peter 2:9)

The most important people in the world are God's people. It's true that without them the gospel would have no voice, society would have no living epistle of God's love, and the world would have no testimony of hope. But this is not what makes them the most important. They are the most important people in the world because they are "the Beloved of God", "a chosen generation". They are as Zechariah states, the "apple of His (God's) eye".

The Christian's sense of being "special" is a mountain not a bubble. In a day when they are about the only minority that are denied the freedom to speak out, God's people need to be reminded of their source of true worth, and with heads held high declare the values and truth of God's Word, regardless of unpopularity.

Personal Notes:

October 12
Hebrews 11:23-29

By faith Moses, when he was born, was hidden three months by his parents, because they saw he was a beautiful child; and they were not afraid of the king's command. By faith Moses, when he became of age, refused to be called the son of Pharaoh's daughter, choosing rather to suffer affliction with the people of God than to enjoy the passing pleasures of sin, esteeming the reproach of Christ greater riches than the treasures in Egypt; for he looked to the reward. By faith he forsook Egypt, not fearing the wrath of the king; for he endured as seeing Him who is invisible. By faith he kept the Passover and the sprinkling of blood, lest he who destroyed the firstborn should touch them. By faith they passed through the Red Sea as by dry land, whereas the Egyptians, attempting to do so, were drowned.

Loving the Harmful

"Raccoons", says Gary Richmond, "go through a glandular change at about 24 months. After that they often attack their owners". The medical records across our own province give sufficient evidence of the dangers of keeping these animals of the wild as pets. Nevertheless, all too often a caring animal lover gets injured by "pet" raccoon. It would seem that people find it difficult to believe that the things they love can be harmful.

The Bible defines sin in a similar way. Regarding the commitment of Moses, Scripture states: "He chose to be ill-treated along with the people of God rather than to enjoy the pleasures of sin for a short time" (Hebrews 11:25 NIV). Indeed, mankind loves the pleasures of sin, even though death is the result: "but each one is tempted when, by his own evil desire, he is dragged away and enticed. Then, after desire has conceived, it gives birth to sin; and sin, when it is full-grown, gives birth to death." (James 1:14-15 NIV). Although death here encompasses the physical and spiritual, James emphasis is on the eternal nature of death which destines a person to everlasting separation from God.

Charles Stanley reminds the reader, "God's only answer to the problem of sin is Jesus Christ. No one can save himself, nor is a person "good" enough to get into heaven. One day each of us will stand before God and give an account of why He should allow us to enter His kingdom... Only God's saving grace through a personal experience with Jesus Christ is the answer to mankind's sin."

Moses chose to love God and find life, more than to love the pleasures of sin which bring eternal death. Each person must likewise make their own choice. God made his desire clear: "The Lord is not slow in keeping his promise, as some understand slowness. He is patient with you, not wanting anyone to perish, but everyone to come to repentance" (2 Peter 3:9 NIV).

The sin that we love will destroy us, God offers a life-giving alternative: "For God so loved the world that he gave his one and only Son, that whoever believes in him shall not perish but have eternal life. For God did not send his Son into the world to condemn the world, but to save the world through him. Whoever believes in him is not condemned, but whoever does not believe stands condemned already because he has not believed in the name of God's one and only Son. This is the verdict: Light has come into the world, but men loved darkness instead of light because their deeds were evil" (John 3:19 NIV). What will your choice be, the pleasures of sin, or life in Christ?

Personal Notes:

October 13
Luke 17:12-29

Then as He entered a certain village, there met Him ten men who were lepers, who stood afar off. And they lifted up their voices and said, "Jesus, Master, have mercy on us!" So when He saw them, He said to them, "Go, show yourselves to the priests." And so it was that as they went, they were cleansed. And one of them, when he saw that he was healed, returned, and with a loud voice glorified God, and fell down on his face at His feet, giving Him thanks. And he was a Samaritan. So Jesus answered and said, "Were there not ten cleansed? But where are the nine?" "Were there not any found who returned to give glory to God except this foreigner?" And He said to him, "Arise, go your way. Your faith has made you well."

The Path to Thankfulness

The family gathered around the table in the traditional Thanksgiving fashion and father returned thanks to God for all His provision. As the meal progressed, father began grumbling about the high cost of living. To this his sweet daughter replied: "I wonder if God will believe your prayer of thanks or complaint of costs!"

Have you ever wondered what makes a truly thankful heart? Luke suggests an answer: "As he (Jesus) was going into a village, ten men who had leprosy met him. They stood at a distance and called out in a loud voice, "Jesus, Master, have pity on us!" When he saw them, he said, "Go, show yourselves to the priests." And as they went, they were cleansed. One of them, when he saw he was healed, came back, praising God in a loud voice. He threw himself at Jesus' feet and thanked him..." (Luke 17:12-16 NIV)

The path to a truly thankful heart has five steps: It begins with the step of an understood condition, all ten men knew their state of leprosy - they stood at a distance! The second step involves an unrestrained cry. All these men pleaded for Jesus to show mercy. They were not ashamed to ask God for help. The third step is much more difficult, it requires an unconditional commitment. Jesus bid them go to the priest for examination before they saw any evidence of healing. Others had been healed instantly, but for these men, this test of commitment was in order, and all were healed on the way.

Now you would think that a grateful heart would be expressed by all ten men who had been healed, but that was not the case. Only one took the fourth step of unselfish consideration. Only one, "when he saw that he had been healed, turned back." Although all had been healed, only one focused his thoughts on the healer. Nine saw the gift of restored health, only one saw the giver. Nine experienced the blessing, only one remembered the benefactor. One alone, proceeded to the final step on the path to a truly grateful heart, the step of undaunted confession: "He glorified God with a loud voice, and fell on his face in worship."

Here is the expression of a truly grateful heart. Here is true thanksgiving: a heart so overjoyed with the God of mercy and grace that the voice must sing His praise and the heart must bow in worship.

And now, to all who know the God of grace and mercy through faith in Christ as Saviour, Paul points to the final steps of a truly thankful heart: "Therefore, I urge you, brothers, in view of God's mercy, to offer your bodies as living sacrifices, holy and pleasing to God--this is your spiritual act of worship" (Romans 12:1 NIV). Do you have a grumbling heart or a truly grateful heart?

Personal Notes:

October 14

Genesis 6:5-14, 11, 16

Then the LORD saw that the wickedness of man was great in the earth, and that every intent of the thoughts of his heart was only evil continually. And the LORD was sorry that He had made man on the earth, and He was grieved in His heart. So the LORD said, "I will destroy man whom I have created from the face of the earth, both man and beast, creeping thing and birds of the air, for I am sorry that I have made them." But Noah found grace in the eyes of the LORD. This is the genealogy of Noah. Noah was a just man, perfect in his generations. Noah walked with God. And Noah begot three sons: Shem, Ham, and Japheth. The earth also was corrupt before God, and the earth was filled with violence. So God looked upon the earth, and indeed it was corrupt; for all flesh had corrupted their way on the earth. And God said to Noah, "The end of all flesh has come before Me, for the earth is filled with violence through them; and behold, I will destroy them with the earth. "Make yourself an ark of gopherwood... ... all the fountains of the great deep were broken up, and the windows of heaven were opened... ...So those that entered [the ark], male and female of all flesh, went in as God had commanded him; and the LORD shut him in.

Societies Slip into the Slough

The "Starweek TV Magazine" graphically summarized a previous season's prime time television as "flush with vulgar language and gross behaviour." The only surprise was that it took so long for them to notice. The reality of our society is that "rude and crude" sells! A quick glance through most newspapers will reveal just how far our "cultured civilization" is removed from being either civilized or cultured. Any casual observer could readily assess our values as "whatever the imagination can cook up, society will swallow."

This is strikingly familiar to a time in history when God assessed earth dwellers by these words: "The LORD saw how great man's wickedness on the earth had become, and that every inclination of the thoughts of his heart was only evil all the time" (Genesis 6:5 NIV). The result of that assessment was a judgement of cataclysmic proportions: "So the LORD said, "I will wipe mankind, whom I have created, from the face of the earth--men and animals, and creatures that move along the ground, and birds of the air" (Genesis 6:7 NIV).

Judgement came as a world flood. Only Noah, his immediate family and a reproducing representative of all species, was saved in the ark that Noah built. Many today look at this report from scripture as a story to illustrate God's anger at sin.

However, the evidence of such a universal flood can not be dismissed, as Dr. Morris suggests in "The Genesis Flood": "The present widely accepted system of uniformitarianism in historical geology, with its evolutionary basis and bias, has been shown to be utterly inadequate to explain most of the important geological phenomena... Some form of catastrophism is clearly indicated by the vast evidences of volcanism, diastrophism, glaciation, coal and oil and mineral deposits, fossilization, vast beds of sediments, and most of the other dominant features of the earth's crust." Only a "violent and rapid activity and formation" such as a world flood could account for the evidence.

"But what does the fact of the flood's reality have to do with me?" you might ask. Everything! According to God: "the world that then was, being overflowed with water, perished: But the heavens and the earth, which are now, by the same word are kept in store, reserved unto fire against the day of judgment and perdition of ungodly men." (2 Peter 3:5-7).

If crudeness is any indication, God's judgement is soon coming, this time by fire. As God gave Noah instructions that he and his family might be saved, so He has given a message of salvation to all mankind today: "God did not appoint us to suffer wrath but to receive salvation through our Lord Jesus Christ. He died for us so that... we may live together with him." (1 Thessalonians 5 NIV). "Everyone who calls on the name of the Lord will be saved." (Romans 10:13 NIV). The hand of God will close the "ark of salvation" once again. Are you safely entered in?

Personal Notes:

October 15
2 Samuel 5: 3-10

Therefore all the elders of Israel came to the king at Hebron, and King David made a covenant with them at Hebron before the LORD. And they anointed David king over Israel. David was thirty years old when he began to reign, and he reigned forty years. In Hebron he reigned over Judah seven years and six months, and in Jerusalem he reigned thirty-three years over all Israel and Judah.
And the king and his men went to Jerusalem against the Jebusites, the inhabitants of the land, who spoke to David, saying, "You shall not come in here; but the blind and the lame will repel you," thinking, "David cannot come in here." Nevertheless David took the stronghold of Zion (that is, the City of David). Now David said on that day, "Whoever climbs up by way of the water shaft and defeats the Jebusites (the lame and the blind, who are hated by David's soul), he shall be chief and captain." Therefore they say, "The blind and the lame shall not come into the house." Then David dwelt in the stronghold, and called it the City of David. And David built all around from the Millo and inward. So David went on and became great, and the LORD God of hosts was with him.

Environment for Vision

Two imprisoned men look out through the same bars; One sees the mud, and one sees the stars. What is it that could make such a difference in perspective? The answer is VISION. Vision has been defined as "hope with a blue print," "the art of seeing the invisible." It is the screen of the mind in which the aspirations of the future are projected. By any definition, vision is very important. It is instrumental in achieving purpose and is essential to Christian ministry. Oliver Wendell Holmes said: "A moment's insight is sometimes worth a life's experience."

With this in mind, a review of 1 Samuel 5: will grant an understanding of the environment for vision: "All the tribes of Israel came to David at Hebron and said, "We are your own flesh and blood. In the past, while Saul was king over us, you were the one who led Israel on their military campaigns. And the LORD said to you, `You shall shepherd my people Israel, and you shall become their ruler.'"

When the elders of Israel came to King David at Hebron, he made a compact before the LORD with them. Upon their anointing of David as king over Israel, he presented a plan to capture Jerusalem and make it the capital (2 Samuel 5:1-3 NIV). Three unique features of this environment spawned this VISION.

First, there was *a sense of camaraderie through relationship*. As the elders gathered before David they declared: "we are thy bone and thy flesh". In essence they were claiming the privilege of all belonging to the same family. This amounted to an expressed desire to bury the past with its unbecoming division and be joined in unity.

Next, there was *a sense of confidence through reputation*. "In time past ... you led us ... out and in". In this, all Israel acknowledged God's call of David to the throne. Israel suddenly remembered that David had stood against Goliath, and David had restored the families from the Amalekites, and David had led the soldiers to recover Saul's body along with Jonathan's for their proper burial. In so remembering David's faithfulness to the Lord, their confidence in him was restored.

Lastly, Israel had *a sense of commitment to responsibility*. David made a covenant with Israel's elders and military leaders. All the people accepted their own responsibility in the covenant as the context goes on to show.

These three ingredients created the environment for discovering the vision of Jerusalem as the city of David. This is the most significant city in all history, and the place from which Christ shall one day reign. Camaraderie, confidence and commitment, these are the ingredients necessary to establish a vision for the Lord's work. To the extent that a local church achieves this environment, it too will find its own vision for God's work. Christ said: "go and make disciples of all nations, baptising them ... and teaching them ..." (Matthew 28:19-20 NIV). Has your church a vision for this work of Christ?

Personal Notes:

October 16
Jeremiah 4:10-18

Then I said, "Ah, Lord GOD! Surely You have greatly deceived this people and Jerusalem, Saying, 'You shall have peace,' Whereas the sword reaches to the heart." At that time it will be said To this people and to Jerusalem, "A dry wind of the desolate heights blows in the wilderness Toward the daughter of My people—Not to fan or to cleanse— A wind too strong for these will come for Me; Now I will also speak judgment against them." "Behold, he shall come up like clouds, and his chariots like a whirlwind. His horses are swifter than eagles. Woe to us, for we are plundered!" O Jerusalem, wash your heart from wickedness, that you may be saved. How long shall your evil thoughts lodge within you? For a voice declares from Dan And proclaims affliction from Mount Ephraim: "Make mention to the nations, Yes, proclaim against Jerusalem, That watchers come from a far country And raise their voice against the cities of Judah. Like keepers of a field they are against her all around, Because she has been rebellious against Me," says the LORD. "Your ways and your doings have procured these things for you. This is your wickedness, Because it is bitter, Because it reaches to your heart."

The Derelict of Bitterness

There is a port on the Canadian side of Lake Erie that is postcard pretty. I used to enjoy visiting this quiet little piece of God's beautiful creation. However, I remember one old fishing scow that was left to rust and rot right at the harbour entrance. For years this rat-infested bucket of bolts marred the entire beauty of that harbour until initiative was taken to tow the scow out into deep water and sink it out of sight.

That scenario is also a picture of the heart of some Christians. What we allow to moor in the harbour of our heart will drastically affect the beauty and value of our lives. The prophet Jeremiah made reference to just such a circumstance: "O Jerusalem, wash your heart from wickedness, that you may be saved. How long shall thy vain thoughts lodge within thee? ...Thy way and thy doings have procured these things unto thee; this is thy wickedness, because it is bitter, because it reaches unto your heart" (Jeremiah 4:14, 18).

Israel had allowed wickedness to harbour in their heart, pride, jealousy, anger, greed and unforgiveness had been allowed to go unchecked in their lives. They had slipped as a people whose words had changed from: "All that the Lord has spoken we will do" (Exodus 19:8), to "I am", "I deserve", "I hate", "I want", and "I will hold on to".

In their rebellion and disobedience to God, Israel had paralleled Satan's self-interest who sinned saying: "I will ascend into heaven, I will exalt my throne above the stars of God: I will sit also upon the mount of the congregation, in the sides of the north: I will ascend above the heights of the clouds; I will be like the most High." (Isaiah 14:13-14).

Israel's wickedness lodged in their heart, and became a rusty derelict of bitterness, spoiling the very beauty of their God-designed creation. Such a root of bitterness produces the fruit of gossip, the fruit of criticism, and the fruit of destruction: "Looking diligently lest any man fail of the grace of God; lest any root of bitterness springing up trouble you, and thereby (you) many be defiled" (Hebrews 12:15).

If the harbour of our heart has become marred with the derelict of bitterness, God calls for cleansing: "If we confess our sins, he is faithful and just to forgive us [our] sins, and to cleanse us from all unrighteousness" (1 John 1:9). Whether pride, jealousy, anger, greed, or unforgiveness, these sins must be confessed and covered by the blood of Christ. Until such cleansing takes place, God's people cannot be the harbours of beauty - the examples of godliness, that He intends believers to be. Christian friend, what is the condition of the harbour of your heart?

Personal Notes:

October 17
Daniel 4:33-37

That very hour the word was fulfilled concerning Nebuchadnezzar; he was driven from men and ate grass like oxen; his body was wet with the dew of heaven till his hair had grown like eagles' feathers and his nails like birds' claws. And at the end of the time I, Nebuchadnezzar, lifted my eyes to heaven, and my understanding returned to me; and I blessed the Most High and praised and honoured Him who lives forever: For His dominion is an everlasting dominion, And His kingdom is from generation to generation. All the inhabitants of the earth are reputed as nothing; He does according to His will in the army of heaven And among the inhabitants of the earth. No one can restrain His hand Or say to Him, "What have You done?" At the same time my reason returned to me, and for the glory of my kingdom, my honour and splendour returned to me. My counsellors and nobles resorted to me, I was restored to my kingdom, and excellent majesty was added to me. Now I, Nebuchadnezzar, praise and extol and honour the King of heaven, all of whose works are truth, and His ways justice. And those who walk in pride He is able to put down.

Christian Gratitude

"Blessed be the God and Father of our Lord Jesus Christ, who hath blessed us with all spiritual blessings in heavenly places in Christ" (Ephesians 1:3). Gratitude, it has been said, is the memory of the heart. In our materialistic society, where there is never "enough", only a striving for "more", the Christian should stand out as one possessing a true sense of gratitude for the blessings from God!

A.W. Tozer in the book "The Best of Tozer" captures the essence of true Christian thanksgiving: "Perhaps it would help us to understand if we thought of ourselves as fish in a vast river, at once enjoying the full flow of the stream, remembering with gratitude the current that has passed and awaiting with joyous anticipation the fullness that is moving on us from upstream. While this is but an imperfect figure of speech, it is quite literally true that we who trust in Christ are borne along by present grace while we remember with thankfulness the goodness we have enjoyed in days past and look forward in happy expectation to the grace and goodness that yet awaits us.

Bernard of Clairvaux speaks of a "perfume compounded of the remembered benefits of God." Such fragrance is too rare. Every follower of Christ should be redolent of such perfume; for have we not all received more from God's kindness than our imagination could have conceived before we knew Him and discovered for ourselves how rich and how generous He is?

That we have received of His fullness, grace for grace, no one will deny; but the fragrance comes not from the receiving; it comes from the remembering, which is something quite different indeed. Ten lepers received their health; that was the benefit. One came back to thank his benefactor; that was the perfume. Unremembered benefits, like dead flies, may cause the ointment to give forth a stinking aroma.

Remembered blessings, thankfulness for present favours and praise for promised grace blend like myrrh and aloes and cassia to make a rare bouquet for the garments of the saints. With this perfume David also anointed his harp and the hymns of the ages have been sweet with it.

Perhaps it takes a purer faith to praise God for unrealized blessings than for those we once enjoyed or those we now enjoy. Yet many have risen to that sunlit peak, as did Anna Waring when she wrote "Glory to Thee for all the grace I have not tasted yet."

Believers are exhorted to: "Rejoice evermore. Pray without ceasing. In every thing give thanks: for this is the will of God in Christ Jesus concerning you." (1 Thessalonians 5:16-18). Christian gratitude keeps life from sagging because there is someone underneath life! Christian friend, let the world see true thankfulness!

Personal Notes:

October 18
1 Peter 2:11-23

Beloved, I beg you as sojourners and pilgrims, abstain from fleshly lusts which war against the soul, having your conduct honourable among the Gentiles, that when they speak against you as evildoers, they may, by your good works which they observe, glorify God in the day of visitation. Therefore submit yourselves to every ordinance of man for the Lord's sake, whether to the king as supreme, or to governors, as to those who are sent by him for the punishment of evildoers and for the praise of those who do good. For this is the will of God, that by doing good you may put to silence the ignorance of foolish men— as free, yet not using liberty as a cloak for vice, but as bondservants of God. Honour all people. Love the brotherhood. Fear God. Honour the king. Servants, be submissive to your masters with all fear, not only to the good and gentle, but also to the harsh. For this is commendable, if because of conscience toward God one endures grief, suffering wrongfully. For what credit is it if, when you are beaten for your faults, you take it patiently? But when you do good and suffer, if you take it patiently, this is commendable before God. For to this you were called, because Christ also suffered for us, leaving us an example, that you should follow His steps: "Who committed no sin, Nor was deceit found in His mouth"; who, when He was reviled, did not revile in return; when He suffered, He did not threaten, but committed Himself to Him who judges righteously.

Increased Disrespect

Now that the Roberto Alamar incident has long since passed from front page, (I refer to Alamar's spitting at the baseball umpire); perhaps its time to reflect on this incident from a personal perspective! As much as behaviour like this is still unacceptable, the disrespect that was evident in the incident toward the authority on the field is evident everywhere in our society. Whether toward police or politicians, clergy or clerks, teachers or tax collectors, blatant disrespect for appointed authority is epidemic in North America.

In the homes of our society there is a regular serving up of roast leaders. With unabashed and unchecked fervour, complaint, criticism and complete undermining of integrity toward all manner of appointed officials takes the forefront of conversations in home and office. Parents are "out to lunch", preachers are "out of touch", teachers are "out to get", and police are "out of control", and as the complaints increase, the respect decreases.

In every area of authority there are "bad apples", just as there are bad attitudes in every area of society. Nevertheless, the continued verbal abuse directed toward appointed authority has lead to an unhealthy acceptance of disrespect in our society. By self-centred arrogance society has undermined the positions of authority and spat upon the people in authority.

In opposition to this epidemic of disrespect, God's Truth cries out: "Submit yourselves to every ordinance of man for the Lord's sake: whether it be to the king, as supreme; Or unto governors, as unto them that are sent by him for the punishment of evildoers, and for the praise of them that do well. For so is the will of God (1 Peter 2:13-15), "Let every soul be subject unto the higher powers. For there is no power but of God: the powers that be are ordained of God. Whosoever therefore resists the power, resists the ordinance of God: and they that resist shall receive to themselves damnation" (Romans 13:1-2).

Could it be that the root of society's disrespect for authority is its disrespect for God? Is it not true that the real reason for society's acceptance of Secular Humanism, along with its atheist foundation and presupposition of evolution, is a total disregard for God, and desire to remove any thought of accountability to the Sovereign Lord? Scripture suggests so: "And even as they did not like to retain God in their knowledge, God gave them over to a reprobate mind, to do those things which are not fitting... Backbiters, haters of God, despiteful, proud, boasters, inventors of evil things, disobedient to parents..."(Romans 1:28, 30). If society spits in the face of God, is it any wonder that its athletes spit in the face of umpires?

For the Christian, God gives a special call. Although requiring an acceptance of vulnerability, by faith the believer is challenged to: "as free, and not using your liberty for a cloak for vice, but as the servants of God. Honour all people. Love the brotherhood. Fear God. Honour the king" (1 Peter 2:16-17).

Personal Notes:

October 19
Psalm 51:1-10

Have mercy upon me, O God, According to Your lovingkindness; According to the multitude of Your tender mercies, Blot out my transgressions. Wash me thoroughly from my iniquity, And cleanse me from my sin. For I acknowledge my transgressions, And my sin is always before me. Against You, You only, have I sinned, And done this evil in Your sight—That You may be found just when You speak, And blameless when You judge. Behold, I was brought forth in iniquity, And in sin my mother conceived me. Behold, You desire truth in the inward parts, And in the hidden part You will make me to know wisdom. Purge me with hyssop, and I shall be clean; Wash me, and I shall be whiter than snow. Make me hear joy and gladness, That the bones You have broken may rejoice. Hide Your face from my sins, And blot out all my iniquities. 0 Create in me a clean heart, O God, And renew a steadfast spirit within me.

A Good Wash

There are probably few who know that itchy, crawly feeling of prickly chaff and scratchy dust mingled with sweat that grinds into your skin better than a farm boy. No one would welcome a cleansing stream and refreshing pool nor appreciate the gentle scrub of soap more! Nevertheless, it was not for want of physical cleansing that David, the former farm boy turned king, cried out to be washed. No, King David had a deeper need, a more uncomfortable and weighty feeling of uncleanness of soul.

Yes, David - the man after God's own heart, felt the great burden of His sin of adultery and murder sweep over him like a wave of the sea, the undertow of which pulled him down into the depths of despair, and separated him from the fellowship and blessing of God. Though he succeeded in keeping his sin from the eyes of men, he could not escape the eye of the living God. Upon rebuke from Nathan, the prophet of the Lord, David's will was broken and his spirit crushed. He cried: "Have mercy upon me, O God, according to thy lovingkindness: according unto the multitude of thy tender mercies blot out my transgressions. Wash me thoroughly from mine iniquity, and cleanse me from my sin... Purge me with hyssop, and I shall be clean: wash me, and I shall be whiter than snow" (Psalms 51:1-2,7).

When man looks upon his life in comparison to fellowman, he justifies himself and excuses his sin, after all, "everybody does it!" However, when brought into proximity to Holy God, man sees his own uncleanliness, grieves his own sin, and cries "I want to be washed!" When Moses approached the burning bush possessed by the presence of God, he became aware of the Holy ground he tread upon. When Isaiah saw the Lord high and lifted up, he understood that he was a man of unclean lips. When the woman at the well confronted Jesus, she became convicted of her immoral life.

There is need for all men to be washed for "all have sinned and come short of the glory of God" (Romans 3:23). David, sensing the weight of his sin, knew the answer lay in the lovingkindness of God. As scripture bears witness: "God commends his love toward us, in that, while we were yet sinners, Christ died for us." (Romans 5:8)

In answer to man's cry, "I want to be washed", God provides a cleansing stream, as William Cowper penned so long ago: "There is a fountain filled with blood, Drawn from Immanuel's veins, and sinners plunged beneath that flood, Lose all their guilty stains: The dying thief rejoiced to see, That fountain in his day, and there may I, though vile as he, Wash all my sins away." Like David, may this be your earnest prayer to God: "I want to be washed!"

Personal Notes:

October 20
Acts 11:19-26

Now those who were scattered after the persecution that arose over Stephen travelled as far as Phoenicia, Cyprus, and Antioch, preaching the word to no one but the Jews only. But some of them were men from Cyprus and Cyrene, who, when they had come to Antioch, spoke to the Hellenists, preaching the Lord Jesus. And the hand of the Lord was with them, and a great number believed and turned to the Lord. Then news of these things came to the ears of the church in Jerusalem, and they sent out Barnabas to go as far as Antioch. When he came and had seen the grace of God, he was glad, and encouraged them all that with purpose of heart they should continue with the Lord. For he was a good man, full of the Holy Spirit and of faith. And a great many people were added to the Lord. Then Barnabas departed for Tarsus to seek Saul. And when he had found him, he brought him to Antioch. So it was that for a whole year they assembled with the church and taught a great many people. And the disciples were first called Christians in Antioch.

The Gift of Encouragement

Wilfred Paterson in "The Art of Living" made this statement: "Words of encouragement fan the spark of genius into the flame of achievement. Legend tells us that Lincoln's mother called her small son to her bedside and whispered, "Be somebody, Abe!" There is perhaps nothing more stimulating to human endeavour than the encouragement of fellow man. Perhaps that is why God said of Adam, "It is not good that the man should be alone."

The book of Acts records the story of a man named Joses who so manifested the qualities of encouragement that the apostles called him Barnabas (which means 'son of encouragement'). Scripture reveals some of the qualities that made him such an encouragement to others. First, he expressed the spirit of sacrifice in giving up his very valuable land, selling it to help others (Acts 4:37). Secondly, when all the apostles mistrusted Saul, Barnabas expressed love in accepting Saul, even though he placed himself in a vulnerable position to do so (Acts 9:26-27). Thirdly, Barnabas stood by Saul, leading him into fellowship until he had turned the tide in Saul's favour (Acts 9:27-28). Fourthly, Barnabas buried the prevalent bigotry against gentiles and reached out to help the believers in Antioch when few other Jewish Christians would consider joining a Gentile congregation (Acts 11:22-24).

Finally, when Barnabas realized his own limitations in teaching the believers at Antioch, he humbly sent for Paul to carry out the work, even to the point of turning the leadership over to Paul (Acts 11:25-26; 13). Barnabas was not without weakness, nevertheless, he manifested such selflessness and unconditional love that his life was defined as Son of Encouragement!

Lawrence Crabb Jr., in his book "Encouragement: The Key to Caring" defines Christian encouragement as "the kind of expression that helps someone want to be a better Christian, even when life is rough". Encouragement is so important to the life of the church that one of the Spiritual gifts (a divine endowment of a special ability upon accepting Jesus as personal saviour) God gives to believers is encouragement. This is translated "exhortation" in Romans 12:6-8 and refers to the ability to draw another individual to oneself and effectively comfort, encourage and provoke to Godly choices, and righteous living.

The obvious prerequisite of being an encourager is to be in contact with people as scripture urges: "Not forsaking the assembling of ourselves together, as the manner of some is; but exhorting (encouraging) one another" (Hebrews 10:25). Christians in particular, have great potential for encouraging one another because of their unique privilege in Christ, in whom they have unconditional acceptance, invaluable assurance and an invincible association, "being knit together in love" (Colossians 2:2).

God's simple plan for encouragement is for His people to invest their efforts in others, for God's glory. This means to strengthen others with prayer, bless others with love, and stir others with hope. Christian friend, are you an encourager in the truest sense of God's desire?

Personal Notes:

October 21
Luke 4:14-21

Then Jesus returned in the power of the Spirit to Galilee, and news of Him went out through all the surrounding region. And He taught in their synagogues, being glorified by all. So He came to Nazareth, where He had been brought up. And as His custom was, He went into the synagogue on the Sabbath day, and stood up to read. And He was handed the book of the prophet Isaiah. And when He had opened the book, He found the place where it was written: "The Spirit of the LORD is upon Me, Because He has anointed Me To preach the gospel to the poor; He has sent Me to heal the brokenhearted, To proclaim liberty to the captives And recovery of sight to the blind, To set at liberty those who are oppressed; To proclaim the acceptable year of the LORD." Then He closed the book, and gave it back to the attendant and sat down. And the eyes of all who were in the synagogue were fixed on Him. And He began to say to them, "Today this Scripture is fulfilled in your hearing."

The Sin of Sodomy

According to The Toronto Star of October 10, 1997 Mayor Dianne Haskett and the city of London were fined for not declaring a "Gay Pride Day". The mayor was quoted as saying: "If this ruling is left unchallenged, any Canadian can be forced to say what they don't believe." The issue, according to the news article was one of "rights"; city officials against that of a small group.

Whether city officials were forced to act against their beliefs, or whether the gay rights movement won or lost the day, is not the final issue! If the Bible is the Word of God and therefore, an expression of God's absolute truth, (and I truly believe it is), the ultimate issue will be accountability to Him. To this end Scripture makes no apology. Whether popular or not, God's Word defines homosexuality ("sodomy" in Scripture) as a sin to be confessed and a lifestyle to be repented of.

The Old Testament denounces sodomy: "Thou shalt not lie with mankind, as with womankind: it is abomination" (Leviticus 18:22), "There shall be no whore of the daughters of Israel, nor a sodomite of the sons of Israel" (Deuteronomy 23:17, see also the book of 1 Kings). The New Testament denounces sodomy: "Be not deceived: neither fornicators, nor idolaters, nor adulterers, nor effeminate, nor abusers of themselves with mankind... shall inherit the kingdom of God. (1 Corinthians 6:9-10).

The clearest passage of scripture which assesses the sin of homosexuality is Romans 1:26-27: "For this cause God gave them up unto vile affections: for even their women did change the natural use into that which is against nature: And likewise also the men, leaving the natural use of the woman, burned in their lust one toward another; men with men working that which is unseemly, and receiving in themselves that recompense of their error which was meet. And even as they did not like to retain God in their knowledge, God gave them over to a reprobate mind, to do those things which are not fitting" (Romans 1:28).

Here seven points of condemnation are enumerated. Homosexuality, as God describes it, involves: ignored parameters (vile affections), abandoned purpose (natural use), selfish passion (burned in lust), disgraceful profanity (unseemly), divine penalty (recompense), sexual perversion (their error), and denounced propriety (doing those things not fitting).

It makes no difference whether man denies God's Word, or plays hermeneutical games in an attempt to remove its application, God has promised that He will judge according to His Word: "He that rejects me, and receives not my words, has one that judges him: the word that I have spoken, the same shall judge him in the last day" (John 12:48).

The wonder in all this is that whether in bondage to the sin of homosexuality, or adultery, or even gluttony, Christ has died to bear the punishment for man's sin and risen again to offer life and strength to break the bondage and set the prisoner free (see John 3:16-17). God gives new life to those who call upon His name.

Personal Notes:

October 22
Matthew 9:35-38

And Jesus went about all the cities and villages, teaching in their synagogues, and preaching the gospel of the kingdom, and healing every sickness and every disease among the people. But when he saw the multitudes, he was moved with compassion on them, because they fainted, and were scattered abroad, as sheep having no shepherd. Then saith he unto his disciples, The harvest truly is plenteous, but the labourers are few; Pray ye therefore the Lord of the harvest, that he will send forth labourers into his harvest.

Life's Emptiness

"I have had few difficulties, many friends, great successes; I have gone from wife to wife, and from house to house, visited great countries of the world, but I am fed up with inventing devices to fill up twenty-four hours of the day." This was the content of the suicide note left by Ralph Barton, cartoonist. There is within the heart of every human an emptiness that can only be filled by God. The filling of this emptiness is the essence of eternal life as Scripture states: "And this is life eternal, that they might know thee the only true God, and Jesus Christ, whom thou hast sent" (John 17:3).

It was this emptiness that led Nicodemus to seek Jesus. Here is his story: "Now there was a man of the Pharisees named Nicodemus, a member of the Jewish ruling council. He came to Jesus at night and said, "Rabbi, we know you are a teacher who has come from God. For no-one could perform the miraculous signs you are doing if God were not with him." In reply Jesus declared, "I tell you the truth, no-one can see the kingdom of God unless he is born again."

"How can a man be born when he is old?" Nicodemus asked. "Surely he cannot enter a second time into his mother's womb to be born!" Jesus answered, "I tell you the truth, no-one can enter the kingdom of God unless he is born of water and the Spirit. Flesh gives birth to flesh, but the Spirit gives birth to spirit. You should not be surprised at my saying, `You must be born again.' The wind blows wherever it pleases. You hear its sound, but you cannot tell where it comes from or where it is going. So it is with everyone born of the Spirit."

"How can this be?" Nicodemus asked.

"You are Israel's teacher," said Jesus, "and do you not understand these things? I tell you the truth, we speak of what we know, and we testify to what we have seen, but still you people do not accept our testimony. I have spoken to you of earthly things and you do not believe; how then will you believe if I speak of heavenly things? No-one has ever gone into heaven except the one who came from heaven--the Son of Man. Just as Moses lifted up the snake in the desert, so the Son of Man must be lifted up, that everyone who believes in him may have eternal life" (John 3:1-15 NIV).

As Nicodemus discovered, being religious does not answer man's emptiness, nor does trying to be good enough to meet God's approval. This eternal life that Jesus speaks of is a gift from God granted by grace to all who acknowledge their own personal sin and permanent separation from God, and who, by faith, believe Jesus died on the cross to take their place of judgement and rose again to offer forgiveness and life. The avenue to life is simple confession and personal trust: "He that believeth on him is not condemned: but he that believeth not is condemned already, because he hath not believed in the name of the only begotten Son of God" (John 3:18).

"The spiritual poverty of the Western world is much greater than the physical poverty of our people. You in the West have millions of people who suffer such terrible loneliness and emptiness". (Mother Teresa). John chapter nineteen suggests that Nicodemus found his emptiness answered in Jesus. Have you?

Personal Notes:

October 23

Romans 3:9-20

What then? Are we better than they? Not at all. For we have previously charged both Jews and Greeks that they are all under sin. As it is written: "There is none righteous, no, not one; There is none who understands; There is none who seeks after God. They have all turned aside; They have together become unprofitable; There is none who does good, no, not one." "Their throat is an open tomb; With their tongues they have practiced deceit"; "The poison of asps is under their lips"; "Whose mouth is full of cursing and bitterness." "Their feet are swift to shed blood; Destruction and misery are in their ways; And the way of peace they have not known." "There is no fear of God before their eyes." Now we know that whatever the law says, it says to those who are under the law, that every mouth may be stopped, and all the world may become guilty before God. Therefore by the deeds of the law no flesh will be justified in His sight, for by the law is the knowledge of sin.

Lost or Found

Most have read about and some have actually experienced the anxiety of having a missing child. You wait beside the phone with nervousness and growing apprehension. The minutes seem like hours and hours like eternities. The heart pounds, the stomach churns, and the only release is hearing from your child.

We've listened to news reports about little ones wondering off, becoming hopelessly lost and perishing with exposure. We've seen the frantic searches for missing children of entire communities and the resulting emotional collapse of strangers, caught up in these searches with a deep empathy for the families. "Lost" is a word that strikes fear to a family as readily as "cancer" to a patient.

God feels such agony for a world of humanity that has turned its back on Him. He aches for the inevitable end, eternal separation of men and women from Him. For this cause He has offered a ready rescue in His Son: "He himself bore our sins in his body on the tree, so that we might die to sins and live for righteousness; by his wounds you have been healed" (1 Pet. 2:24). To all who by faith would turn to Him for salvation (deliverance from eternal separation), God's anxiety is turned to the delight of a Father united with a prodigal child: "For you were like sheep going astray, but now you have returned to the Shepherd and Overseer of your souls" (1 Peter 2:25).

Like the child who wonders into the woods after a scurrying squirrel, oblivious to the danger and ignorant of any sense of direction, so the great obstacle of human nature is the lack of understanding and admission of being lost. Johann Paul Friedrich Richter (1763-1825) accurately described the lost state of man: "No one is so much alone in the universe as a denier of God. With an orphaned heart, which has lost the greatest of fathers, he stands mourning by the immeasurable corpse of the universe."

Yet, as Oswald Chambers states in *He Shall Glorify Me*: "Our Lord begins where we would never begin, at the point of human destitution. The greatest blessing a man ever gets from God is the realization that, if he is going to enter into His Kingdom, it must be through the door of destitution. Naturally we do not want to begin there; that is why the appeal of Jesus is of no use until we come face to face with realities; then the only One worth listening to is the Lord."

God continues to extend His love and grace: "But God demonstrates his own love for us in this: While we were still sinners, Christ died for us" (Romans 5:8 NIV). For those who accept this provision of rescue, there is rejoicing in heaven: "I say unto you, that likewise joy shall be in heaven over one sinner that repents" (Luke 15:7). To such God promises: "I will never leave you nor forsake you" (Hebrews 13:5).

Dear reader, are you lost or found?

Personal Notes:

October 24
Ephesians 6:1-4

Children, obey your parents in the Lord, for this is right. "Honour your father and mother," which is the first commandment with promise: "that it may be well with you and you may live long on the earth." And you, fathers, do not provoke your children to wrath, but bring them up in the training and admonition of the Lord.

Loving Discipline

There is a renewed tune afoot that, like the fabled pied piper's tune, will lead our children to destruction. The words to this tune are "thou shalt not spank thy child lest he become psychologically scarred." In a world where child abuse is so prevalent, it is understandable that extra caution must be taken. Nevertheless, God declares the outcome of such a philosophy: "The rod and reproof give wisdom: but a child left to himself brings his mother to shame" (Proverbs 29:15).

The Bible uses such terms as "train up a child", "provoke not your children to wrath", and "withhold not correction." God has definite ideas about rearing children. When carefully investigated, God's Word reveals a definite plan for child discipline:

Step One is to <u>Establish Guilt</u>. Godly discipline follows a sense of guilt. The child must know the wrong done. This establishes a relationship between the wrong deed and the need for punishment and reinforces the fact that doing wrong again will bring correction.

Step two is to <u>Establish Authority</u>. Show the child that discipline is a responsibility God gave parents to exercise. "Chasten thy son while there is hope, and let not thy soul spare for his crying" (Proverbs 19:18). The child must come to see parents under God's authority just as children are under parents' authority.

Step three is to <u>Establish Love</u>. Discipline is never to be done apart from a spirit of love. Child abuse would never occur if parents practised discipline in love. God is our perfect model: "...whom the Lord loves he corrects; even as a father the son in whom he delights." (Proverbs 3:12). Tell children before disciplining them that you are doing this because you love them. They in turn will identify correction as an act of love.

Step four is to <u>Exercise Discipline</u>. Following these steps allows discipline to be done purposefully and deliberately without anger. "He that spares his rod hates his son: but he that loves him chastens him betimes" (Proverbs 13:24). Discipline should hurt more than enjoyment of wrong! Spanking should involve the least amount of force to break the child's will but not the spirit, exercised with care, not anger.

The final step involves <u>Encouraged Fellowship</u>. An act of disobedience breaks the fellowship between a parent and child. Now that discipline has been exercised and the child has paid for his disobedience, the parent needs to re-establish fellowship. Double punishment (spanking and sending to their room) sends the wrong message. Have a word of prayer. Tell your child you love him. Provide comfort by giving him a hug. Put the wrong behind by acting with true forgiveness, as though it never happened.

Parents must keep their word about discipline and exercise it well each time a wrong occurs. Although it may seem burdensome, the result of Godly discipline is obedient and respectful children. Proper discipline makes a child better, not bitter and is a beautiful picture of God's relationship to believers in taking their punishment for sin and offering true forgiveness, as though it never happened.

Personal Notes:

October 25
Deuteronomy 6:4-12

"Hear, O Israel: The LORD our God, the LORD is one! "You shall love the LORD your God with all your heart, with all your soul, and with all your strength. "And these words which I command you today shall be in your heart. "You shall teach them diligently to your children, and shall talk of them when you sit in your house, when you walk by the way, when you lie down, and when you rise up. "You shall bind them as a sign on your hand, and they shall be as frontlets between your eyes. "You shall write them on the doorposts of your house and on your gates. "So it shall be, when the LORD your God brings you into the land of which He swore to your fathers, to Abraham, Isaac, and Jacob, to give you large and beautiful cities which you did not build, "houses full of all good things, which you did not fill, hewn–out wells which you did not dig, vineyards and olive trees which you did not plant—when you have eaten and are full— "then beware, lest you forget the LORD who brought you out of the land of Egypt, from the house of bondage.

Parenting Styles

What's the best way to raise a child so he'll be both happy and competent? Psychologist Diana Baumrind of the University of California at Berkley studied three groups of nursery school children. The parents of one group were permissive, undemanding, insecure about how to influence their children, not well organized in running their households, somewhat warm toward the kids, but tending to baby them. A second group of parents were authoritative. They ran better-coordinated households, set clear rules and gave reasons, demanded a good deal but were consistent, loving and secure in handling their children and trained them in independence. The third group were "authoritarian." They exerted firm control and used power freely but showed little affection. They gave no reasons for their directives except perhaps "an absolute moral imperative," and they did not encourage kids to express themselves when they disagreed.

You guessed it. The parents who followed the middle course were the most successful. The children of the authoritarian parents were less content, more insecure and apprehensive, more likely to become hostile, under stress. Kids with permissive parents were dependent, immature, while the most competent and mature of all were the kids of authoritative -- that is, firm and demanding but loving and understanding parents. Their children were self-reliant, self-controlled, realistic, able to get along with others, eager to explore.

This is exactly the pattern set forth in the Bible for parents to follow: "Train up a child in the way he should go: and when he is old, he will not depart from it" (Proverbs 22:6). Here, the responsibility of the parent is to develop in the child a hunger, a taste or desire for good, upright, moral and spiritual things, bringing the child to the place where he personally desires to partake of such things himself. "And, ye fathers, provoke not your children to wrath: but bring them up in the nurture and admonition of the Lord" (Ephesians 6). Here, the parent is responsible for "nurturing:" discipline and instruction that establishes parameters of behaviour and exercises discipline when broken, and "admonition:" counsel and direction from God's Word that brings an understanding of why there are parameters in life.

Susannah Wesley, for example, spent one hour each day praying for her 17 children. In addition, she took each child aside for a full hour every week to discuss spiritual matters. No wonder two of her sons, Charles and John, were used of God to bring blessing to all of England and much of America. Here are a few rules she followed in training her children: "(1) Subdue self-will in a child and thus work together with God to save his soul. (2) Teach him to pray as soon as he can speak. (3) Give him nothing he cries for and only what is good for him if he asks for it politely. (4) To prevent lying, punish no fault which is freely confessed, but never allow a rebellious, sinful act to go unnoticed.
(5) Commend and reward good behaviour. (6) Strictly observe all promises you have made to your child."

Personal Notes:

October 26
Psalm 36:1-12

Your mercy, O LORD, is in the heavens; Your faithfulness reaches to the clouds. Your righteousness is like the great mountains; Your judgments are a great deep; O LORD, You preserve man and beast. How precious is Your lovingkindness, O God! Therefore the children of men put their trust under the shadow of Your wings. They are abundantly satisfied with the fullness of Your house, And You give them drink from the river of Your pleasures.
For with You is the fountain of life; In Your light we see light. Oh, continue Your lovingkindness to those who know You, And Your righteousness to the upright in heart. Let not the foot of pride come against me, And let not the hand of the wicked drive me away. There the workers of iniquity have fallen; They have been cast down and are not able to rise.

Satisfaction

The story is told of a farmer who had lived on the same farm all his life, but with the passing years, the farmer began to tire of it. Every day he found a new reason for criticizing some feature of the old place. Finally, he decided to sell, and listed the farm with a real estate broker who promptly prepared a sales advertisement. As one might expect, it emphasized all the farm's advantages: ideal location, modern equipment, healthy stock, acres of fertile ground, etc. Before placing the ad in the newspaper, the realtor called the farmer and read the copy to him for his approval. When he had finished, the farmer cried out, "Hold everything! I've changed my mind. I am not going to sell. I've been looking for a place like that all my life.

In our society, satisfaction caries a million dollar price tag with no guarantee and no money back offer! The proverbial pursuit of life, liberty, and happiness that is supposed to spell "satisfaction" escapes most. This is not because of poor effort, but because of misunderstanding of satisfaction's source.

Oswald Chambers said: "The man or woman who does not know God demands an infinite satisfaction from other human beings which they cannot give, and in the case of the man, he becomes tyrannical and cruel. It springs from this one thing, the human heart must have satisfaction, but there is only one Being Who can satisfy the last abyss of the human heart, and that is the Lord Jesus Christ."

Psalm 103:5 says, "He satisfies my desires with good things, so that my youth is renewed like the eagles." The eagle is a symbol of strength and beauty, and, for the ancient Hebrew, new life! Because the eagle molts (sheds and regrows) all its feathers annually, it represented to the Hebrew prophets the gift of renewed life found in the living Lord. This, Paul referred to in Romans 12:2: "Do not be conformed to this world, but be ye transformed by the renewing of your mind."

The beauty of the Christian experience is the promise of God to continue a process of change in the believer; producing godly character, refining the thinking process, redirecting values and priorities, and establishing a deep sense of purpose and well-being. Paul reminds the believer to be "confident of this very thing, that He who has begun a good work in you will complete it until the day of Jesus Christ." (Philippians 1:6).

"God has set Eternity in our heart, and man's infinite capacity cannot be filled or satisfied with the things of time and sense." (F.B. Meyer). Only a relationship with God through faith in Jesus Christ can truly bring satisfaction to the soul. George MacDonald said it simply: "When, with all the loved around thee, Still, thy heart says, "I am lonely." It is well; the truth has found thee: Rest is with the Father only." Friend, have you found the source of satisfaction?

Personal Notes:

October 27
Psalm 85:1-13

LORD, You have been favorable to Your land; You have brought back the captivity of Jacob. You have forgiven the iniquity of Your people; You have covered all their sin. Selah You have taken away all Your wrath; You have turned from the fierceness of Your anger. Restore us, O God of our salvation, And cause Your anger toward us to cease. Will You be angry with us forever? Will You prolong Your anger to all generations? Will You not revive us again, That Your people may rejoice in You? Show us Your mercy, LORD, And grant us Your salvation. I will hear what God the LORD will speak, For He will speak peace To His people and to His saints; But let them not turn back to folly. Surely His salvation is near to those who fear Him, That glory may dwell in our land. Mercy and truth have met together; Righteousness and peace have kissed. Truth shall spring out of the earth, And righteousness shall look down from heaven. Yes, the LORD will give what is good; And our land will yield its increase. Righteousness will go before Him, And shall make His footsteps our pathway.

Search for Peace

Amos Elon in 'The New Yorker' (Dec. 24, 1990) wrote: "The feeling of being beset by blind forces is especially strong in the mixed city of Jerusalem. ... Hardly a day passes in the "holy city" without a riot or a stoning, without cars being torched or firebombs thrown, without attempted lynchings or the stabbing of an Israeli by a Palestinian (or vice versa). After each incident, municipal cleaning machines, marked "CITY OF PEACE" in three languages, appear on the scene to wash the blood from the streets." Peace is something the world is desperately in need of. Historians tell us that there are more wars going on now than ever before. All the efforts of modern man cannot engineer peace among nations when there is no peace within the human heart.

A friend of mine, working just outside Jerusalem recently sent this letter: "On Saturday morning, for the first time in 3 years, we had a major conflict on our street. The Moslems threw rocks, screaming, "God is greater". Six Israeli jeeps of soldiers were protecting our street as we headed out to our Sabbath Meeting. The soldiers responded by firing teargas canisters at regular intervals.

While all this was going on, just below our fence in our yard, an elderly Moslem shepherd had gathered his sheep around him during all the commotion. I went to the edge of our fence and saw him there. We greeted each other in Arabic. Every time the guns fired tear gas, the sheep jumped and were afraid. The shepherd never stopped talking softly to his sheep. He reached out with his staff constantly touching each sheep very gently. Several of the other sheep a few meters away ran to the shepherd when the guns fired. The shepherd was talking to me in Arabic, but was totally unaffected by what was going on just 200 meters down the way. This picture of God's dealing encouraged us amidst all of our conflicts and difficulties. Just like it is written in Psalm 23, He truly is an oasis of calm and rest when evil men and problems surround us: "Thy rod and staff they comfort me."

My friend has pointed to an important fact; in order to find peace, there must be a relationship with the Prince of Peace – Jesus Christ. To know Him is to know the good shepherd who died to provide PEACE WITH GOD through faith in His sacrifice (Romans 5:1), and rose again to offer THE PEACE OF GOD, the inner ministry of the Holy Spirit whereby God produces the fruit of peace in a life (Galatians 5:22). Jesus said: "My sheep hear my voice, and I know them, and they follow me" (John 10:27). "True peace is not merely the absence of some negative force, tension or war, it is the presence of some positive force, justice, good will, brotherhood." That force is a person, God's own son, the Lord Jesus Christ Jesus. He invites all to believe in His name and find life and peace

Personal Notes:

October 28
2 Corinthians 6:11-7:1

O Corinthians! We have spoken openly to you, our heart is wide open. You are not restricted by us, but you are restricted by your own affections. Now in return for the same (I speak as to children), you also be open. Do not be unequally yoked together with unbelievers. For what fellowship has righteousness with lawlessness? And what communion has light with darkness? And what accord has Christ with Belial? Or what part has a believer with an unbeliever? And what agreement has the temple of God with idols? For you are the temple of the living God. As God has said: "I will dwell in them And walk among them. I will be their God, And they shall be My people." Therefore "Come out from among them And be separate, says the Lord. Do not touch what is unclean, And I will receive you." "I will be a Father to you, And you shall be My sons and daughters, Says the LORD Almighty."

Therefore, having these promises, beloved, let us cleanse ourselves from all filthiness of the flesh and spirit, perfecting holiness in the fear of God.

Come to the Garden

As parents enjoy the company of their children so God enjoys fellowship with man. God came, "walking in the garden in the cool of the day" (Genesis 3:8), to fellowship with His children. Unfortunately, sin separated Adam and Eve from that wonderful fellowship. In their shame they "hid themselves from the presence of the Lord" (Genesis 3:8). In order to restore fellowship, God provided a sacrifice, clothing Adam and Eve with the skin of that sacrifice, teaching that atonement (covering) for sin was innocent blood. Nevertheless, the consequences of their action passed on to all mankind. By virtue of procreation, sin nature is inherited by all, leaving everyone estranged from the Lord: "For there is not a just man on earth who does good And does not sin" (Ecclesiastes 7:20), "for all have sinned and fall short of the glory of God" (Romans 3:23).

It is in this context that the name 'Immanuel' offers so much hope and encouragement. This name of God literally means 'God with us' and is used of the promise of the coming of the Saviour: "Therefore the Lord Himself will give you a sign: Behold, the virgin shall conceive and bear a Son, and shall call His name Immanuel."

(Isaiah 7:14). The joy of salvation is the offering of Jesus Christ, God's Son as a once for all sacrifice of innocent blood for sin. A sacrifice that does not just "cover" for sin, but "washes" sin away, leaving the believer "as white as snow" (Isaiah 1:18). This forgiveness and cleansing restores the wonder of God's fellowship with man: "But if we walk in the light as He is in the light, we have fellowship with one another, and the blood of Jesus Christ His Son cleanses us from all sin." (1 John 1:7), "As God has said: "I will dwell in them and walk among them. I will be their God, and they shall be My people." (2 Corinthians 6:16). To all who have believed, Paul makes this appeal: "Therefore, having these promises, beloved, let us cleanse ourselves from all filthiness of the flesh and spirit, perfecting holiness in the fear of God." (2 Corinthians 7:1).

A certain man wanted to sell his house. Another man wanted to buy it, but because he was poor, he couldn't afford the full price. The owner agreed to sell the house for half the original price with just one stipulation: he would retain ownership of one small nail protruding over the door.

After several years, the original owner wanted the house back, so he found the carcass of a dead dog, and hung it from the nail he still owned. Soon the house became unliveable and the family was forced to sell back. Paul's appeal was simply for Christians to realize that if the Devil is left with even one small peg in life, he will return to hang his rotting garbage on it, making it unfit for Christ's habitation, spoiling the privilege of fellowship.

Friend, do you frequent God's garden?

Personal Notes:

October 29
1 Corinthians 15:3-11

For I delivered to you first of all that which I also received: that Christ died for our sins according to the Scriptures, and that He was buried, and that He rose again the third day according to the Scriptures, and that He was seen by Cephas, then by the twelve. After that He was seen by over five hundred brethren at once, of whom the greater part remain to the present, but some have fallen asleep. After that He was seen by James, then by all the apostles. Then last of all He was seen by me also, as by one born out of due time. For I am the least of the apostles, who am not worthy to be called an apostle, because I persecuted the church of God. But by the grace of God I am what I am, and His grace toward me was not in vain; but I labored more abundantly than they all, yet not I, but the grace of God which was with me. Therefore, whether it was I or they, so we preach and so you believed.

The Greatest of the Great

Mankind has a fascination for "the greatest," that's why the Guinness Book of Records is so popular! This theme is evident in Scripture as well. Christ was asked about the "greatest commandment", Paul spoke of love as the "greatest" virtue among faith, hope and love, and in the book of Hebrews the reader is urged not to neglect "so great a salvation." It is here that I wish to stop and ask: "Do you know what is the greatest thing about salvation?"

There are seven great things mentioned about salvation in Ephesians 2: 8-9: "For by grace you have been saved through faith, and that not of yourselves; it is the gift of God, not of works, lest anyone should boast." There is first the *Ground* of Salvation – "GRACE" – getting something that is not deserved. Because man continually disobeys God, he deserves the judgment of God. Salvation is the acquittal of that judgment because Christ took mans place in judgment. Next there is the *Character* of Salvation – "GIFT" – receiving something not earned. Because of man's propensity for sin, he cannot overcome guilt nor tip the balance of wrongs by doing right; justice prohibits this. Salvation is granted as a free gift, given out of love. Tere is also the *Means* (channel) of Salvation – "FAITH" – man's response to the truth of God's offer of salvation. God asks only that individuals would admit their personal sin before Him and believe that His Son, Jesus Christ, paid the debt of sin by dying on the cross and conquered the power of sin by rising from the dead. This faith is expressed in confession of sin and acceptance of the gift of life God offers. The text identifies the *Deliverance* of Salvation – "SAVED" – the Bible term for escaping the judgment of God upon sin. Scriptures teach that deliverance is a result of being; *redeemed* – Jesus paid the price of man's sin, *justified* – declared innocent of wrong doing, *forgiven* – guilt removed and sin forgotten. This text speaks also of the *Condition* of Salvation – "NOT OF OURSELVES" – the admission that man can never improve himself to be morally acceptable before God. This leads to the *Comfort* of Salvation "NOT OF WORKS" – the removal of the burden of trying to meet God's standard of perfection and the worry of wondering if there is yet something that must be done to satisfy God.

All these are great truths about salvation, but the greatest truth is *The Wonder of Salvation:* "by grace YOU have been saved." This is the wonder that salvation is personal, that God Wants Me! Although God is self – sufficient, He desires a real relationship with every person. God's heart is so great with love that God wants me, and God wants you!

In 1995, Christopher Reeve, the "Superman" actor, was paralyzed from the shoulders down. In the days which followed both he and his mother considered pulling the plug on his life support system. But his wife, through tears, persuaded him to fight back, saying, "I want you to know that I will be with you for the long haul, no matter what. You're still you, and I love you." The greatest thing about salvation is God saying "You're still you, and I love you and I want you."

Personal Notes:

October 30
John 11:18-27

Now Bethany was near Jerusalem, about two miles away. And many of the Jews had joined the women around Martha and Mary, to comfort them concerning their brother. Then Martha, as soon as she heard that Jesus was coming, went and met Him, but Mary was sitting in the house. Then Martha said to Jesus, "Lord, if You had been here, my brother would not have died. "But even now I know that whatever You ask of God, God will give You." Jesus said to her, "Your brother will rise again." Martha said to Him, "I know that he will rise again in the resurrection at the last day." Jesus said to her, "I am the resurrection and the life. He who believes in Me, though he may die, he shall live. "And whoever lives and believes in Me shall never die. Do you believe this?" She said to Him, "Yes, Lord, I believe that You are the Christ, the Son of God, who is to come into the world."

Dead Bones can Live

With the prominence of skeletons decorating so many homes this Halloween season, Ezekiel's vision might be appropriate to consider: "The hand of the LORD was upon me, and he brought me out by the Spirit of the LORD and set me in the middle of a valley; it was full of bones. He led me to and fro among them, and I saw a great many bones on the floor of the valley, bones that were very dry. He asked me, "Son of man, can these bones live?" I said, "O Sovereign LORD, you alone know." Then he said to me, "Prophesy to these bones and say to them, `Dry bones, hear the word of the LORD! This is what the Sovereign LORD says to these bones: I will make breath enter you, and you will come to life. I will attach tendons to you and make flesh come upon you and cover you with skin; I will put breath in you, and you will come to life. Then you will know that I am the LORD.'" So I prophesied as I was commanded. And as I was prophesying, there was a noise, a rattling sound, and the bones came together, bone to bone. I looked, and tendons and flesh appeared on them and skin covered them, but there was no breath in them. Then he said to me, "Prophesy to the wind (breath); prophesy, son of man, and say to it, `This is what the Sovereign LORD says: Come from the four winds, O breath, and breathe into these slain, that they may live.'" So I prophesied as he commanded me, and breath entered them; they came to life and stood up on their feet--a vast army." (Ezekiel 37:1-10 NIV)

Although the text clearly addresses God's promise to restore the nation Israel, (a promise yet to be fulfilled), Ezekiel's vision is a portrait of God's process of individual spiritual renewal. Christ called this being "born again" (John 3), and scripture confirms that this involves two agencies: First, the working of the Word of God: "For you have been born again, not of perishable seed, but of imperishable, through the living and enduring Word of God" 1 Peter 1:23. This is evident in the text above as Ezekiel's prophecies. Secondly, the ministry of the Spirit of God as Jesus stated, "I tell you the truth, no-one can enter the kingdom of God unless he is born of water and the Spirit" John 3:5, (this is evident in Ezekiel 37 as breath entering, bringing life).

Salvation is so unique that scripture defines it as new birth (John 3), new creation (2 Cor. 5:17), new life ("quickened" in Eph. 2:1), and pictures it as the dead coming to life. The texts of Scripture reveal that it is all of God: "For it is by grace you have been saved, through faith--and this not from yourselves, it is the gift of God-- not by works, so that no-one can boast" (Ephesians 2 NIV).

Are you a bag of bones or a picture of Spiritual life?

Personal Notes:

October 31
John 17:1-10

Jesus spoke these words, lifted up His eyes to heaven, and said: "Father, the hour has come. Glorify Your Son, that Your Son also may glorify You, "as You have given Him authority over all flesh, that He should give eternal life to as many as You have given Him. "And this is eternal life, that they may know You, the only true God, and Jesus Christ whom You have sent. "I have glorified You on the earth. I have finished the work which You have given Me to do. "And now, O Father, glorify Me together with Yourself, with the glory which I had with You before the world was. "I have manifested Your name to the men whom You have given Me out of the world. They were Yours, You gave them to Me, and they have kept Your word. "Now they have known that all things which You have given Me are from You. "For I have given to them the words which You have given Me; and they have received them, and have known surely that I came forth from You; and they have believed that You sent Me. "I pray for them. I do not pray for the world but for those whom You have given Me, for they are Yours. "And all Mine are Yours, and Yours are Mine, and I am glorified in them.

God's Desire

Jesus said that He came to offer abundant life. This can be defined as a passion for a person, the pursuit of God Himself. It is being in a relationship with the Lord where God makes Himself uniquely real every day. Israel's entrance into the promised land as described in the book of Joshua, is a graphic portrayal of the believer's pursuit of this abundant life. As well, a study in Israel's Journey to Jordan evidences the apparent Obstacles to The Pursuit of the Abundant Life, the first of which is *failing to see God's earnest desire to lead His people to abundance*. For example, God's willing heart is evident in Exodus where: He is willing to bless many for the faith of few (Ex. 1:17-21), He is willing to agonize His people to bring forth a leader (Ex. 1:22 – 2:22), He is willing to invoke His promises when His own cry out (Ex.2:23-25), He is willing to uniquely reveal Himself to equip His leadership (Ex.3:2), He is willing to patiently wait for His leadership to come around (Ex.4), He is willing to magnify the burden of bondage upon His people in order to convince that His is the only path to freedom,

(Ex. 5:5-9) and where He is willing to destroy the strength of a nation to demonstrate His sovereign power and the uniqueness of His people (Ex.3:19-29, chapters 7 – 14).

The measure of God's passion for His people to enjoy abundance is clear in His willingness to "move mountains" and invoke struggle to achieve it. The same is true today. God's desire is for His own to enjoy the abundant life in Christ. Failing to see this passion is failing to see God's own continuing love for those who have received Christ. Although accepting Christ as Saviour is accepting God's love by believing that "God demonstrated His own love toward us in that while we were yet sinners Christ died for us" (Romans 5:8). It is characteristic of humanity to either doubt the continuation of that love because of difficult circumstances, or become complacent to that continuing love through the routine of religion! In either event, the constant reminder of God's unwavering, unconditional, unending love, is the greatest motivator toward pursuit of a deepening relationship with the living God who has promised: "He who has My commandments and keeps them, it is he who loves Me. And he who loves Me will be loved by My Father, and I will love him and show Myself to him" (John 14:21).

Abbe Henri de Tourville (1842-1903) once wrote: "As for that which is beyond your strength, be absolutely certain that our Lord loves you, devotedly and individually, loves you just as you are.... Accustom yourself to the wonderful thought that God loves you with a tenderness, a generosity, and an intimacy that surpasses all your dreams. Give yourself up with joy to a loving confidence in God and have courage to believe firmly that God's action toward you is a masterpiece of partiality and love. Rest with tranquility in this abiding conviction."

Personal Notes:

November 1
1 Thessalonians 1:6-2:12

And you became followers [imitators] of us and of the Lord, having received the word in much affliction, with joy of the Holy Spirit, so that you became examples to all in Macedonia and Achaia who believe. For from you the word of the Lord has sounded forth, not only in Macedonia and Achaia, but also in every place. Your faith toward God has gone out, so that we do not need to say anything. For they themselves declare concerning us what manner of entry we had to you, and how you turned to God from idols to serve the living and true God, and to wait for His Son from heaven, whom He raised from the dead, even Jesus who delivers us from the wrath to come. For you yourselves know, brethren, that our coming to you was not in vain. But even after we had suffered before and were spitefully treated at Philippi, as you know, we were bold in our God to speak to you the gospel of God in much conflict. For our exhortation did not come from error or uncleanness, nor was it in deceit. But as we have been approved by God to be entrusted with the gospel, even so we speak, not as pleasing men, but God who tests our hearts. For neither at any time did we use flattering words, as you know, nor a cloak for covetousness—God is witness. Nor did we seek glory from men, either from you or from others, when we might have made demands as apostles of Christ. But we were gentle among you, just as a nursing mother cherishes her own children. So, affectionately longing for you, we were well pleased to impart to you not only the gospel of God, but also our own lives, because you had become dear to us. For you remember, brethren, our labor and toil; for laboring night and day, that we might not be a burden to any of you, we preached to you the gospel of God. You are witnesses, and God also, how devoutly and justly and blamelessly we behaved ourselves among you who believe; as you know how we exhorted, and comforted, and charged every one of you, as a father does his own children, that you would walk worthy of God who calls you into His own kingdom and glory.

The labour of a "Follower" of Christ

The greatest respect is due the pantomime artist who studies the many body movements and facial expressions necessary to imitate the simplest action. This requires hours of hard work. Yet this kind of work should not be unfamiliar to the Christian. In 3 John 11, the believer is exhorted to "follow not that which is evil, but that which is good." The word translated 'follow' is the word "mimeomai". The English words mime, mimic, and mimeograph are derived from this Greek word. This word translated in modern text as 'follow' or 'imitate', expresses the idea of examining, reflecting back to something clearly identified, and then actually copying that characteristic in one's own life.

Paul called the Corinthians to "imitate Himself as He imitated Christ." (1 Corinthians 11:1). Indeed, Paul's chief aim in life was to "know Christ, and the power of His resurrection, and the fellowship of His suffering, being conformed to His death." (Philippians 3:10).

To follow Christ <u>begins</u> with placing our faith <u>in</u> His sacrificial death on the cross in punishment for our sins and His resurrection from the dead for our justification. However, this is <u>only</u> a beginning. As the pantomime artist studies body movements and facial expression in order to imitate actions, so must the believer study the character and qualities of Christ as revealed in scripture, and seek by the power of the Holy Spirit, to imitate these qualities. In the popular Christian novel "In His Steps", Charles Sheldon, the author captures this concept with a story suggesting the impact of a few Christians on a town when every decision they make is preceded by the question "What would Jesus do?" This is a very practical way of imitating Christ.

Every Christian is called upon to do the work of the pantomime artist in studying and imitating Jesus. Only in so doing can one truly say he is a "follower of Christ." To this end every believer is also called to 1Th 2:14 "became imitators of the churches of God which are in Judea in Christ Jesus. For you also suffered the same things from your own countrymen, just as they did from the Judeans," Heb 6:12 "imitate those who through faith and patience inherit the promises," and 1Peter 3:13 "become followers of what is good". Christian friend, do you work at following?

Personal Notes:

November 2
Psalm 78:1-8

Give ear, O my people, to my law; Incline your ears to the words of my mouth. I will open my mouth in a parable; I will utter dark sayings of old, which we have heard and known, and our fathers have told us. We will not hide them from their children, telling to the generation to come the praises of the LORD, And His strength and His wonderful works that He has done. For He established a testimony in Jacob, And appointed a law in Israel, Which He commanded our fathers, That they should make them known to their children; That the generation to come might know them, The children who would be born, That they may arise and declare them to their children, That they may set their hope in God, And not forget the works of God, But keep His commandments; And may not be like their fathers, A stubborn and rebellious generation, A generation that did not set its heart aright, And whose spirit was not faithful to God.

Sound Home Building

It is an alarming but not surprising fact that in today's society one half of all marriages end in divorce. What often appears to be the very best of beginnings, ends in frustration and separation. The Bible explains the reason for this, scripture says "Except the Lord build the house, they labour in vain that build it." (Psalm 127:1). The importance of the home to society is evidenced in it's establishment during creation: "And the LORD God said, [It is] not good that the man should be alone; I will make him an help meet for him... And the rib, which the LORD God had taken from man, made he a woman, and brought her unto the man... Therefore shall a man leave his father and his mother, and shall cleave unto his wife: and they shall be one flesh (Genesis 2). The home is not a result of an evolutionary process necessitated by the survival of the fittest, but the purposeful design of God as the foundation for society.

The Lord, being the architect of the home, must be central in its construction. In building up of character, in constructing plans for life and work, in framing schemes of happiness, in rearing a hope of eternal life, Christ must be the guide. Scripture states that husbands are to love their wives <u>as the Lord</u> loved the church; wives are to submit to their husbands <u>as unto the Lord;</u> children are to obey their parents <u>in the Lord;</u> fathers are to raise their children in the instruction and discipline <u>of the Lord.</u> It is clear that the building of a home begins with a right relationship with the Lord, where each partner has personally trusted Christ as Saviour, and continues with God's principles for the home being followed.

Jesus compared the individual who hears His word and refuses to practice it to a foolish builder who builds his home on sand. "Therefore whoever hears these sayings of Mine, and does them, I will liken him to a wise man who built his house on the rock: "and the rain descended, the floods came, and the winds blew and beat on that house; and it did not fall, for it was founded on the rock. "But everyone who hears these sayings of Mine, and does not do them, will be like a foolish man who built his house on the sand: "and the rain descended, the floods came, and the winds blew and beat on that house; and it fell. And great was its fall" (Matthew 7:24-28). When the storms come, the house is destroyed. Many homes have been crushed by the storms of frustration, financial pressure, or fear because God's principles were not followed. God's blessing is on the home only to the extent that it's members submit to His precepts. Don't labour in vain. The architect of the home is God; therefore, take time to learn and adopt God's "family principles" and begin to build your home from the eternal materials of God's word.

Personal Notes:

November 3
Galatians 6:1-10

Brethren, if a man is overtaken in any trespass, you who are spiritual restore such a one in a spirit of gentleness, considering yourself lest you also be tempted. Bear one another's burdens, and so fulfill the law of Christ. For if anyone thinks himself to be something, when he is nothing, he deceives himself. But let each one examine his own work, and then he will have rejoicing in himself alone, and not in another. For each one shall bear his own load. Let him who is taught the word share in all good things with him who teaches. Do not be deceived, God is not mocked; for whatever a man sows, that he will also reap. For he who sows to his flesh will of the flesh reap corruption, but he who sows to the Spirit will of the Spirit reap everlasting life. And let us not grow weary while doing good, for in due season we shall reap if we do not lose heart. Therefore, as we have opportunity, let us do good to all, especially to those who are of the household of faith.

Weight Watchers

It would seem, with the overwhelming flood of calorie reduced food and fitness products that the whole world has become weight watchers. As much as being health conscious is good, for the believer in Christ there is another kind of weight watching to consider. Being reminded of Paul's letter to the Galatians, Christians are called upon to be spiritual weight watchers: "Bear ye one another's burdens, and so fulfil the law of Christ". (Galatians 6:2) Here the word burden (bar-os) refers to a heaviness or weight that presses down upon a person, certain troubling circumstances that crush a fellow believer.

The context of Galatians 6 suggests certain sins that a fellow Christian has fallen into which present a burden of circumstances seemingly insurmountable, in which believing friends draw close and out of love help that brother become restored to fellowship with God. This kind of "weight watching" involves a humble expression of love combined with a careful self examination of personal walk with God (Galatians 6:3-4).

The Lord is asking, through Paul, for every believer to be sensitive toward the weaknesses of others, and to carry that sensitivity with active concern as the fulfilment of "the law of

Christ". This law was defined earlier in the epistle: "For, brethren, ye have been called unto liberty; only [use] not liberty for an occasion to the flesh, but by love serve one another. For all the law is fulfilled in one word, [even] in this; Thou shalt love thy neighbour as thyself". (Galatians 5:13-14) It has been stated that Christians are more inclined to shoot their wounded than treat them. Such was not the case with Christ who was willing to forgive the offender upon repentance rather than stone for the offence (John 8:1-11).

In this very same passage, believers are also urged to carry their own weight: "For every man shall bear his own burden". (Galatians 6:5) Here the word burden (for-tee-on) refers to the personal "burden of responsibility" that the Lord lays on each of His followers including this commitment to love. By privilege of new life, every Christian must carry their own God given responsibilities. However, lest any Christian become discouraged by these cares and turn from them, all should remember the words of Christ: "Take my yoke upon you, and learn of me; for I am meek and lowly in heart: and ye shall find rest unto your souls. For my yoke [is] easy, and my burden is light". (Matthew 11). To be a Christian is to be joined (yoked) together with the one in whom all strength and love is found and therefore is to have available through Him the power to perform His work. Paul stated it this way: "I can do all things through Christ which strengthens me." (Philippians 4:13).

To a bell boy, weight is work, to a prospector, weight is wealth, to the believer, weight is both work and wealth. Fellow Christian, be a conscientious weight watcher.

Personal Notes:

November 4
James 3:1-13

My brethren, let not many of you become teachers, knowing that we shall receive a stricter judgment. For we all stumble in many things. If anyone does not stumble in word, he is a perfect man, able also to bridle the whole body. Indeed, we put bits in horses' mouths that they may obey us, and we turn their whole body. Look also at ships: although they are so large and are driven by fierce winds, they are turned by a very small rudder wherever the pilot desires. Even so the tongue is a little member and boasts great things. See how great a forest a little fire kindles! And the tongue is a fire, a world of iniquity. The tongue is so set among our members that it defiles the whole body, and sets on fire the course of nature; and it is set on fire by hell. For every kind of beast and bird, of reptile and creature of the sea, is tamed and has been tamed by mankind. But no man can tame the tongue. It is an unruly evil, full of deadly poison. With it we bless our God and Father, and with it we curse men, who have been made in the similitude of God. Out of the same mouth proceed blessing and cursing. My brethren, these things ought not to be so. Does a spring send forth fresh water and bitter from the same opening? Can a fig tree, my brethren, bear olives, or a grapevine bear figs? Thus no spring yields both salt water and fresh. Who is wise and understanding among you? Let him show by good conduct that his works are done in the meekness of wisdom.

The Tongue of Fire

Canada is a country that knows, too well, the destructive power of a forest fire. One small spark or one carelessly tossed match can result in the loss of life and destruction of property which is immeasurable. There is another kind of destructive power which begins small, yet creates far greater devastation. The Bible says "the tongue is a fire, the world of iniquity, a member which defiles the entire body, and sets on fire the course of our life". (James 3:6). Here, we are reminded that the tongue, understood to represent the very source of our communication, is characterized by sin. In World War II posters reminded soldiers that "Loose Lips Sink Ships"; in the Bible, we are reminded that loose lips wreck lives. Such devastation resulting from uncontrolled tongues has been seen of late from the sports arena to the political arena. The resulting scenes are hardly less vicious than the death scenes of the gladiator arenas.

Though too sophisticated for such gruesome sport, today's society continues to self destruct through the fire of the tongue. By it the whole person is affected by the tongue. Consider the number of families, friendships, jobs and even countries destroyed by the tongue. The number is immeasurable. What the world needs now is tongue-control. Scripture states: "no one can tame the tongue" (James 3:8). This does not mean mankind is without hope. According to this very passage, tongue-control comes through Spirit control.

Scripture reminds us that in order for the Holy Spirit to control a life, an individual must first confess to God that he is a sinner, unable to rescue himself. He must ask Christ, who died for our sins, to enter his life as his Saviour: "That if thou shalt confess with thy mouth the Lord Jesus, and shalt believe in thine heart that God hath raised him from the dead, thou shalt be saved. For with the heart man believeth unto righteousness; and with the mouth confession is made unto salvation" (Romans 10:9-10).

Think for a moment the logic of James' words as he continues: "Doth a fountain send forth at the same place sweet [water] and bitter? Can the fig tree, my brethren, bear olive berries? either a vine, figs? so [can] no fountain both yield salt water and fresh" (James 3:11-12). Then ask yourself; What is more likely to come from my lips, "sweet water" or "bitter"? The answer could indicate the state of your heart. Is it a heart that Christ is able to change? With Christ in a person's life, the Holy Spirit is able to overcome the power of the tongue as the believer sincerely prays "Set a watch O Lord, before my mouth keep the door of my lips"(Psalm 141:3).

Personal Notes:

November 5
Genesis 2:21-25

And the LORD God caused a deep sleep to fall on Adam, and he slept; and He took one of his ribs, and closed up the flesh in its place. Then the rib which the LORD God had taken from man He made into a woman, and He brought her to the man. And Adam said: "This is now bone of my bones and flesh of my flesh; She shall be called Woman, Because she was taken out of Man." Therefore a man shall leave his father and mother and be joined to his wife, and they shall become one flesh. And they were both naked, the man and his wife, and were not ashamed.

Family Foundations: Equality

The Imperial Hotel in Tokyo, Japan survived the great earthquake of 1923, and became a refuge for the survivors of that tragedy. The reason for this hotel's escape was its careful design by architect Frank Lloyd Wright. Knowing the hotel was to rest on fluid ground, he designed the structure to ride out any shock waves by use of a specially engineered foundation. There is another kind of "quake" that is shaking our society and causing great suffering as well. This quake is centred directly in the middle of a vacuum- the absence of moral and ethical integrity, the void of spiritual and social understanding, the abandonment of absolute truth. Because of this vacuum, society is collapsing, taking with it victims from every age and distinction. The only refuge that will survive is that which is designed and created with careful foundation by the all-wise architect, God. That refuge is the family.

With great care and purpose, the Lord God created the family with certain foundational blocks that assure its safety, as long as those blocks are built upon. These foundational blocks are evident in Genesis 1 and 2. The first of these foundational blocks is a recognition of equality between husband and wife. "So God created man in his own image, in the image of God he created him; MALE AND FEMALE HE CREATED THEM. God blessed THEM and said to THEM, "Be fruitful and increase in number; fill the earth and subdue it. Rule over the fish of the sea and the birds of the air and over every living creature that moves on the ground." (Genesis 1:27-28 NIV).

In every sense, Adam and Eve were created equal. In material, they were both created from the particles of earth, Adam from dust, Eve from Adam (Genesis 2). In essence, they both received the special attention of God's personal design (Genesis 2), and were formed with a distinctly superior soul (intellect, emotions, and will) as well as an eternal spirit. In privilege they were equal in their fellowship with God (Genesis 3:8) and equal in their dominion over nature.

With the foundational block of "recognized equality", which had nothing to do with God's designed purpose and role for each, this first family had every opportunity to sustain an environment of sound attitudes between man and women. The entrance of sin and consequent corruption of that "recognized equality" (seen in Genesis 3), has affected every generation since with wrong attitude between the sexes. This has never been more prominent than in our society today. The abandonment of this foundational stone in the building of today's families has left homes susceptible to the "quake".

Howard Hendricks, in his book "Heaven Help the Home", suggests that families are like sand dunes, formed by influences not purposes. Those who desire a strong family, one that can withstand the great quake of today, cannot ignore David's challenge "Except the LORD build the house, they labour in vain that build it:" (Psalms 127:1). Is there an acknowledgement of God designed equality between sexes in your home?

Personal Notes:

November 6
Ecclesiastes 3:1-10

To everything there is a season, A time for every purpose under heaven: A time to be born, And a time to die; A time to plant, And a time to pluck what is planted; A time to kill, And a time to heal; A time to break down, And a time to build up; A time to weep, And a time to laugh; A time to mourn, And a time to dance; A time to cast away stones, And a time to gather stones; A time to embrace, And a time to refrain from embracing; A time to gain, And a time to lose; A time to keep, And a time to throw away; A time to tear, And a time to sew; A time to keep silence, And a time to speak; A time to love, And a time to hate; A time of war, And a time of peace. What profit has the worker from that in which he labors? I have seen the God-given task with which the sons of men are to be occupied.

Thrills and Agony

The thrill of victory and agony of defeat have broader implications than the sports field. Being created in the image of God, man is an emotional being. God says there is: "a time to weep and a time to laugh, a time to mourn and a time to dance" (Ecclesiastes 3:4 NIV). Christians are called to: "Be angry and sin not" (Ephesians 4:26). Emotional responses by God's perfect design can bring deeper understanding of oneself.

Emotions, as windows to our souls, help us see our goals in light of God's goals. Solomon pursued pleasure, wisdom and wealth yet found himself feeling empty. The result was a truer picture of God's goals: "Remember your Creator in the days of your youth, before the days of trouble come and the years approach when you will say, `I find no pleasure in them' ... here is the conclusion of the matter: Fear God and keep his commandments, for this is the whole [duty] of man" (Ecclesiastes 12:1, 13 NIV).

Emotional responses, as echoes of our thinking can help us identify wrong values. Peter's remorse after denying the Lord undoubtedly pointed out his value of personal safety over loyalty to Jesus, a self-revelation that later prompted complete loyalty at the cost of imprisonment and ultimately death. His appeal confirms the lesson learned: "Therefore, since Christ suffered in his body, arm yourselves also with the same attitude, because he who has suffered in his body is done with sin. As a result, he does not live the rest of his earthly life for evil human desires, but rather for the will of God" (1 Peter 4:1-2 NIV).

Emotional response identifies the anthem of our focus. Elisha's servant, seeing the enemy around the town, responded with fear and trepidation, the anthem of his focus was "no help, no hope". Elisha's prayer was answered by the divine enablement of a different focus: the revelation of the protective army of God's angels. The new anthem of God's Help and Hope" became "Great is Thy Faithfulness." Although God made man's emotional framework for unique purposes (only a token of which has been touched on here), man through disobedience has marred that perfect design. The human heart is dark to the creative purpose of emotion because it is dark to God. Dr. Lawrence Crabb, former assistant professor of psychology at the University of Illinois states that "because of man's fall (from God's perfect design), we have emotional problems: We are afraid to face all that we feel and therefore we sometimes pretend that we are not experiencing the emotions which are really occurring within us".

The best of thrill and agony is found in restored life in Christ who declared: "I have come that they may have life, and have it to the full" (John 10:10 NIV).

Personal Notes:

November 7
Acts 4:8-14

Then Peter, filled with the Holy Spirit, said to them, "Rulers of the people and elders of Israel: "If we this day are judged for a good deed done to a helpless man, by what means he has been made well, "let it be known to you all, and to all the people of Israel, that by the name of Jesus Christ of Nazareth, whom you crucified, whom God raised from the dead, by Him this man stands here before you whole. "This is the 'stone which was rejected by you builders, which has become the chief cornerstone.' "Nor is there salvation in any other, for there is no other name under heaven given among men by which we must be saved." Now when they saw the boldness of Peter and John, and perceived that they were uneducated and untrained men, they marvelled. And they realized that they had been with Jesus. And seeing the man who had been healed standing with them, they could say nothing against it.

Only One Way

At the end of his life the great conqueror, Napoleon, expressed the deep emptiness of his own life in these words: "I die before my time and my body shall be given back to the earth and devoured by worms. What an abysmal gulf between my deep miseries and the eternal Kingdom of Christ. I marvel that whereas the ambitious dreams of myself and of Alexander and of Caesar should have vanished into thin air, a Judean peasant -Jesus- should be able to stretch his hands across the centuries, and control the destinies of men and nations." Jesus Christ is unique.

There are many today who for the sake of human peace and harmony promote a multi-faith "Christianity" whereby all religions are accepted as expressions of true worship. In their broad approach, they forsake one of the fundamental claims of Christ. He said: "I am the way and the truth and the life. No-one comes to the Father except through me" (John 14:6 NIV). True Christianity focuses first on man's need to find peace with God: "Therefore, since we have been justified through faith, we have peace with God through our Lord Jesus Christ" (Romans 5:1).

So important was the need for man to regain peace with God the Father that the fundamental purpose of God becoming man was to pay the penalty of sin on man's behalf: "God was reconciling the world to himself in Christ, not counting men's sins against them. And he has committed to us the message of reconciliation ... For God made him who had no sin to be sin for us, so that in him we might become the righteousness of God." (2 Corinthians 5:19,21 NIV).

All people should have the right to worship as they choose, and there are many choices, yet the marked difference between Christianity and other "religions" is this: Jesus alone rose from the dead to confirm that He was God, Jesus alone controls the destinies of nations and is the one who is master of life itself, Jesus alone can fill the void that exists in the human heart without God.

For this reason true Christians must plead with all mankind in earnest expression of their God-given responsibility. "We are therefore Christ's ambassadors, as though God were making his appeal through us. We implore you on Christ's behalf: Be reconciled to God, ... For God so loved the world that he gave his one and only Son, that whoever believes in him shall not perish but have eternal life" (2 Corinthians 5:20 NIV, John 3:16 NIV)

Will you commit your life to Christ and let Him stretch out His hand to you with the gift of eternal life?

Personal Notes:

November 8
Isaiah 40: 27-31

Why do you say, O Jacob, And speak, O Israel: "My way is hidden from the LORD, And my just claim is passed over by my God"? Have you not known? Have you not heard? The everlasting God, the LORD, The Creator of the ends of the earth, neither faints nor is weary. His understanding is unsearchable. He gives power to the weak, And to those who have no might He increases strength. Even the youths shall faint and be weary, And the young men shall utterly fall, But those who wait on the LORD Shall renew their strength; They shall mount up with wings like eagles, They shall run and not be weary, They shall walk and not faint.

God's Supply of Strength

All the truths of scripture are significantly important, yet none more so than this one, four times repeated: "The just shall live by faith" (Habakkuk 2:4, Romans 1:17, Galatians 3:11, Hebrews 10:38). Ron Jensen in *Leadership Magazine* shares an illustration of living by faith. "Leaves use up nutrients in the process of photosynthesis. As the leaves consume nutrients in the sap, a suction is formed, which draws more sap from the roots. Without the sap, the leaves and branches would die. But the continual flow of this sap comes only as it is used by the work of the leaf. Likewise through faith we draw life from Christ. But the continual supply of fresh nutrients depends on our willingness to "consume" the old supply through our acts of obedience, through our works."

Paul referred to this principle when, in the midst of a physical weakness that the Lord chose not to heal, this apostle stated: "... I will boast all the more gladly about my weaknesses, so that Christ's power may rest on me. That is why, for Christ's sake, I delight in weaknesses, in insults, in hardships, in persecutions, in difficulties. For when I am weak, then I am strong" (2 Corinthians 12:9-10 NIV). Paul had learned the secret of the Lord's "supply of strength" - when believers choose to walk by faith, to follow in obedience, to trust implicitly despite circumstances or feared consequences, then that expressed faith draws life from Christ.

This faith is the point of entrance into the family of God: "Yet to all who received him, to those who believed in his name, he gave the right to become children of God - children born not of natural descent, nor of human decision or a husband's will, but born of God." (John 1:12-13 NIV). This walk of faith is the process of growth as a child of God: "For therein is the righteousness of God revealed from faith to faith ." (Romans 1:17). The genuine, initial act of faith, which receives Jesus Christ as personal Saviour, produces the life of faith in manifesting God's righteousness. This righteousness increases in measure as personal preferences give way, by faith, to God's purpose and path.

  The beauty of the Christian life is that the supply of strength never runs out, the leaves never change colour with the season and die. There is always life for faith to draw from: "I have come that they may have life, and have it to the full." said Christ (John 10:10 NIV). However, by choice, the lack of willingness to consume the Lord's supply (choosing to abandon the walk of faith) will greatly diminish the process of growth. This is why so many Christians are only a faded and withered expression of what God intends them to be.

  Is this then not an appropriate question to consider: Friend, how is the sap running?"

Personal Notes:

November 9
2 Peter 1:1-4

Simon Peter, a bondservant and apostle of Jesus Christ, To those who have obtained like precious faith with us by the righteousness of our God and Savior Jesus Christ: Grace and peace be multiplied to you in the knowledge of God and of Jesus our Lord, as His divine power has given to us all things that pertain to life and godliness, through the knowledge of Him who called us by glory and virtue, by which have been given to us exceedingly great and precious promises, that through these you may be partakers of the divine nature, having escaped the corruption that is in the world through lust.

Precious Promises

No merchant or company clerk would file checks paid for their products in a drawer marked "promises", with no intention of cashing these checks. The value of payment in the completion of a transaction is the cashing of the check. The world is full of people who know their earthly wealth by claiming the value of payment checks, yet never consider heavenly riches. Nevertheless, scripture contains a vast storehouse of "exceedingly great and precious promises" (2 Peter 1:4).

In Bunyan's great allegory, *Pilgrim's Progress*, the incident is related of how Christian decides to leave the Main Highway and follow another Path which seemed easier. But this Path leads him into the territory of Giant Despair who owns Doubting Castle. Eventually he is captured by Giant Despair and kept in a dungeon. He is advised to kill himself. The Giant said there was no use trying to keep on with his journey. For the time, it seemed as if Despair had really conquered Christian. But then Hope, Christian's companion, reminds him of previous victories. So it came about that on Saturday about midnight they began to pray, and continued in prayer until almost morning.

Now a little before it was day, good Christian, as one half amazed, broke out in passionate speech, "What a fool am I thus to lie in a stinking Dungeon, when I may as well be at liberty. I have a Key in my bosom called Promise that will, I am persuaded, open any lock in Doubting Castle." Then said Hopeful, "That's good news. Good Brother, pluck it out of thy bosom and try." And the prison gates flew open.

God's promises are not in His Word for the sake of good reading, nor are they there as a point of encouragement to stimulate positive thinking, God's promises are the real avenue to spiritual life, sustenance and hope. Without the promises of God, "living by faith" has no solid ground to tread upon.

And what is the focus of these promises? They point to, and stand upon, the promise made in God's own blood: "For this is my blood of the new testament (promise), which is shed for many for the remission of sins." (Matthew 26:28). The promise of forgiveness and eternal life in Christ are received by faith, entering the believer into a new and meaningful relationship that unfolds all other promises of God.

Charles Spurgeon once wrote: "When father Adam was in business, he became bankrupt and left us nothing but a sea of debt. But then we (Christians) are married to King Jesus, who is heir of all things, and He puts the check book of promises into our hands, that we may draw from the riches of divine grace."

Don't ignore the greatest source of wealth available to humanity - the exceedingly great and precious promises of God.

Personal Notes:

November 10
Philippians 1:12-21

But I want you to know, brethren, that the things which happened to me have actually turned out for the furtherance of the gospel, so that it has become evident to the whole palace guard, and to all the rest, that my chains are in Christ; and most of the brethren in the Lord, having become confident by my chains, are much more bold to speak the word without fear. Some indeed preach Christ even from envy and strife, and some also from good will: The former preach Christ from selfish ambition, not sincerely, supposing to add affliction to my chains; but the latter out of love, knowing that I am appointed for the defence of the gospel. What then? Only that in every way, whether in pretence or in truth, Christ is preached; and in this I rejoice, yes, and will rejoice. For I know that this will turn out for my deliverance through your prayer and the supply of the Spirit of Jesus Christ, according to my earnest expectation and hope that in nothing I shall be ashamed, but with all boldness, as always, so now also Christ will be magnified in my body, whether by life or by death. For to me, to live is Christ, and to die is gain.

Real Life!

Some time ago my son and I went on a last of season camp out. We arrived in the evening on a remote lake in Muskoka, which we had all to ourselves. The dawn of the next day broke fresh, clear and surprisingly warm. As we sat on the shore and watched the sun rise, we found ourselves "breathing deep of the wilderness air". To us, this was life! How easy it is to define life as a pleasurable experience, a breath of wilderness air, a special celebration with the family, a warm fireplace with a good book. The only problem with this definition of life is its dependency upon pleasant happenings. The Lord God offers so much more!

Paul, while under house arrest and chained to a Roman guard, wrote to the believers of Philippi these remarkable words: "For to me, to live is Christ and to die is gain." (Philippians 1:21 NIV). This was not a pretentious statement of courage, nor was it an attempt to put up a good front. The word that Paul used for "living" (dzah'-o) expressed true life worthy of its name. It was fresh, strong, vigorous life, life to its fullest.

What Paul had discovered was that in the hardship of imprisonment for the sake of the gospel ("I am in chains for Christ" Philippians 1 NIV), he found the highest experience of all that life was meant to be. Paul had become completely dependant upon Christ for daily provision, for strength to declare and defend the gospel before Caesar, for courage to carry on when many forsook him (Philippians 1:15-16). This complete dependence on Christ brought a greater dynamic of life, it brought a consuming grace in which Jesus occupied all the attention of Paul's mind, all the devotion of Paul's heart, all the activity of Paul's life.

Paul found what Jesus spoke of to the woman at the well: "If you knew the gift of God ...you would have asked him and he would have given you living (dzah'-o) water" (John 4:10 NIV). Paul had been drinking deeply of that living water and found it more satisfying than any pleasurable happenings, more fulfilling than any personal achievement, more enriching than any human relationship.

In our world, so marred by wickedness and twisted by human depravity, where even "breathing deep of the wilderness" has no lasting value (and is out of reach for most anyway), dzah'o-life can still be found. Charles Spurgeon once said: "We can learn nothing of the gospel except by feeling its truths. There are some sciences that may be learned by the head, but the science of Christ crucified can only be learned by the heart." This is true of the science of "Jesus, the living water" as well, found only through the experience of total dependence upon Him. This opens the door to His consuming grace. No wonder James boldly declared: "Consider it pure joy, my brothers, whenever you face trials of many kinds" (James 1:2 NIV).

Personal Notes:

November 11
Matthew 26:26-30

And as they were eating, Jesus took bread, blessed and broke it, and gave it to the disciples and said, "Take, eat; this is My body." Then He took the cup, and gave thanks, and gave it to them, saying, "Drink from it, all of you. "For this is My blood of the new covenant, which is shed for many for the remission of sins. "But I say to you, I will not drink of this fruit of the vine from now on until that day when I drink it new with you in My Father's kingdom." And when they had sung a hymn, they went out to the Mount of Olives.

Remember

There was a time back in the days of High School cadets that I was privileged to be a part of the colour guard of our corps, leading the cadets in full dress through town to the cenotaph. It seemed as though the whole town stopped its daily routine to participate in the Remembrance Day Ceremony. As part of that prestigious colour guard, we exercised fancy gun drill in special uniform dress while leading the march in the honoured first position. For me it was all the excitement of a hero's welcome.

The march halted and the guard performed the gun drill of a special salute which ended with the team encircling the cenotaph, guns at rest and heads bowed. The drill went off without a hitch, leaving each of us facing this old pillar, hearts beating with excitement and heads bowed for a one minute silence. It was then that I first noticed the names, worn with age yet clear as ever. These were the names, cut deep in the old pillar, of all the people from our town who had died in war for our country. As I read down the long list, I was humbled to tears to think that others fought and died, yet I was basking in their glory. How could I have been so preoccupied that I forgot the real cost of freedom? That was a meaningful learning experience for me in two ways: it helped me appreciate the cost of freedom, and guard against forgetting those who paid the price; it also helped me understand why the Lord gave the church the Remembrance of Communion.

It is so easy to "bask in the glory" of sins forgiven, to enjoy the fellowship of man to God offered freely to all who "believe on the Lord Jesus Christ" (see Romans 10:9-10), and forget with preoccupation, the cost. As believers gather to celebrate Communion, they are brought back to the remembrance of Christ's death on the cross through the symbol of His broken body - the broken bread, and the symbol of His shed blood - the cup of wine. Paul spoke of this time as a declaration and remembrance: "The Lord Jesus, on the night he was betrayed, took bread, and when he had given thanks, he broke it and said, "This is my body, which is for you; do this in remembrance of me." In the same way, after supper he took the cup, saying, "This cup is the new covenant in my blood; do this, whenever you drink it, in remembrance of me." For whenever you eat this bread and drink this cup, you proclaim the Lord's death until he comes. (1 Corinthians 11:23-26 NIV).

    The joy of the Christian remembrance is that Christ rose from the dead to secure that eternal life for all who repent and believe. Nevertheless, in our remembrances let us pay true honour with humble gratitude, where honour is due: to the soldiers who died for their country, to the Saviour who died for the world.

Personal Notes:

November 12
Hebrews 11:1-10

Now faith is the substance of things hoped for, the evidence of things not seen. For by it the elders obtained a good testimony. By faith we understand that the worlds were framed by the word of God, so that the things which are seen were not made of things which are visible. By faith Abel offered to God a more excellent sacrifice than Cain, through which he obtained witness that he was righteous, God testifying of his gifts; and through it he being dead still speaks. By faith Enoch was taken away so that he did not see death, "and was not found, because God had taken him"; for before he was taken he had this testimony, that he pleased God. But without faith it is impossible to please Him, for he who comes to God must believe that He is, and that He is a rewarder of those who diligently seek Him. By faith Noah, being divinely warned of things not yet seen, moved with godly fear, prepared an ark for the saving of his household, by which he condemned the world and became heir of the righteousness which is according to faith. By faith Abraham obeyed when he was called to go out to the place which he would receive as an inheritance. And he went out, not knowing where he was going. By faith he dwelt in the land of promise as in a foreign country, dwelling in tents with Isaac and Jacob, the heirs with him of the same promise; for he waited for the city which has foundations, whose builder and maker is God.

No Place to Go

A number of years ago I had the privilege of being in the Caribbean for a couple of weeks. While there, a friend and I asked to be taken scuba diving, with a research team. The leader of the team was unimpressed with the complement of full equipment in which we were attired. He insisted that we take a test to demonstrate our ability to survive in crisis. This reminds me of many Christians, all dressed up in their Sunday best, with no place to go. I do not refer to attending church; I refer to progressing in Christian life. The Lord can take them no farther in the Christian experience because they have not demonstrated survival skills.

Israel, in Nehemiah's day, was in a similar position. In order to proceed in their relationship with the living God, three important steps were taken: "On the twenty-fourth day of the same month, the

Israelites gathered together, fasting and wearing sackcloth and having dust on their heads. Those of Israelite descent had separated themselves from all foreigners. They stood where they were and read from the Book of the Law of the LORD their God for a quarter of the day, and spent another quarter in confession and in worshipping the LORD their God" (Nehemiah 9 NIV). First, there was an *earnest desire after God*. God will never plant the seed of His life in the soil of a hardened heart. In genuine humility (sackcloth and ashes), and without distraction (separating themselves), the remnant of Israel tuned their hearts to hear and obey the Lord. For half a day, they were absorbed in the Word of God and prayer.

Secondly, there was *personal reflection upon God*. Upon the hearing of the Scriptures, the people pondered God Himself. They contemplated His greatness: "Thou art God alone" (verse 6), they considered His character: "Thou art righteous" (verse 7), they were moved by His love: "But you are a forgiving God, gracious and compassionate, slow to anger and abounding in love."(verse 17). In their reflection upon God they began to count the blessings with which He had favoured them. A heart of gratitude began to swell within the camp.

Out of this heart of gratitude flowed *a genuine commitment to God*: "you (Lord) have acted faithfully, while we did wrong...we are making a binding agreement... all these now join... and bind themselves with a curse and an oath to follow the Law of God."(Nehemiah 9:33,38; 10:29 NIV). Israel confessed their sin and dedicated themselves to simple obedience to God. In essence they determined to "walk by faith".

In the Christian life, "all roads lead to Rome". That Rome is FAITH. Without faith no one can find God (John 14:6), no one can please God (Hebrews 11:6), and no one can follow God (Matthew 16:24). The survival skill required to proceed in Christian life is to walk by faith, trusting in God's Word as guide, and rule for life!

Dear Christian, are you all dressed with no place to go?

Personal Notes:

November 13
1 Thessalonians 4:1-8

Finally then, brethren, we urge and exhort in the Lord Jesus that you should abound more and more, just as you received from us how you ought to walk and to please God; for you know what commandments we gave you through the Lord Jesus. For this is the will of God, your sanctification: that you should abstain from sexual immorality; that each of you should know how to possess his own vessel in sanctification and honour, not in passion of lust, like the Gentiles who do not know God; that no one should take advantage of and defraud his brother in this matter, because the Lord is the avenger of all such, as we also forewarned you and testified. For God did not call us to uncleanness, but in holiness. Therefore he who rejects this does not reject man, but God, who has also given us His Holy Spirit.

The Old Morality

Because corrosion is eating away at the ancient marble, priceless statues in the Acropolis of Athens have been replaced by plaster replicas. Air pollution and the rusting of metal joints used by restorers 50 years ago have caused more damage in the last two decades than the ravages of time in the previous two millennia.

Whether in restoring monuments or building relationships, the "New Age" of enlightenment has little lasting value. This is especially clear with our present day new morality, which accepts premarital sex as well as homosexual relationships. So called "health specialists" advocate a "birth control and safe sex" gospel in which this new ideology suggests to young people "If you feel like you are ready, it's okay, no restraint, no shame, just protect". As a consequence, sexually transmitted diseases are practically epidemic, the divorce rate is higher than ever before and single parenting has become the burden of thousands.

God opposes this new morality: "It is God's will that you should be sanctified: that you should avoid sexual immorality; that each of you should learn to control his own body in a way that is holy and honourable" (1 Thessalonians 4 NIV), "For this reason a man will leave his father and mother and be united to his wife, and the two will become one flesh." (Ephesians 5:31 NIV) "Marriage should be honoured by all, and the marriage bed kept pure, for God will judge the adulterer and all the sexually immoral." (Hebrews 13:4 NIV)

In "A Better Kind of Sex" (Newsweek, July 13, '92) Sharon Sheehan comments on her return to a high school to talk to teens. She states: "Behind their "correct" value-free facade lurks a deep sense of loss. They lament the lack of guidelines and moral structure... It's as if the gap between sex and marriage has opened a huge, empty hole in which there is no real sure thing. A loving relationship that lasts - hasn't that always been the bottom line? Isn't the real 'C word' for sex education commitment, not condoms? It's time to give the thousands of couples who have been happily married 20, 30, 40 years equal access to sex-education classes."

The ancient institution of the family has been, in North America, corroded more in the last decade by loose morality than ever before. Those who have tried to replace it with the cheap imitation of free sex, have left a heritage of self destruction.

Even though God's age old morality is mocked by many, when held on to, it still produces good marriages. After all, the one who designed the family knows best how to keep it: "Unless the LORD builds the house, its builders labour in vain." (Psalm 127:1 NIV).

Personal Notes:

November 14
James 3:13-18

Who is wise and understanding among you? Let him show by good conduct that his works are done in the meekness of wisdom. But if you have bitter envy and self-seeking in your hearts, do not boast and lie against the truth. This wisdom does not descend from above, but is earthly, sensual, demonic. For where envy and self-seeking exist, confusion and every evil thing are there. But the wisdom that is from above is first pure, then peaceable, gentle, willing to yield, full of mercy and good fruits, without partiality and without hypocrisy. Now the fruit of righteousness is sown in peace by those who make peace.

Peace on Earth

Three days have passed, the poppies are gone, the cenotaph is behind and the Christmas tree ahead. The "Lest We Forget" seems already forgotten in the coming rush of the season. Yet war goes on. Every day this past week, war has taken the lives of soldiers and civilians somewhere in our world. Nevertheless, apart from the 15 second news coverage, our thoughts rarely return to the horror of human conflict, especially as the "Season of Christmas" draws near. This serves to show how truly far removed man is from the real meaning and purpose of the Incarnation (God becoming man). The very purpose of Christ's coming was to provide a way to peace. The angels announced His coming as an answer to war: "Glory to God in the highest, and on earth peace, good will toward men" (Luke 2:14). This peace the angels said was a matter of salvation: "For unto you is born this day in the city of David a Saviour, which is Christ the Lord" (Luke 2:11).

Like Humpty Dumpty, who had a great fall, so our world has had a great fall. Paul describes this fall vividly: "Therefore, just as sin entered the world through one man (Adam), and death through sin, and in this way death came to all men, because all sinned" (Romans 5:12 NIV). Adam's wilful disobedience to God left in man the heritage of a sin nature resulting in continued rebellion against God and fellowman.

The sins of self-righteousness and pride toward God, greed and hate toward mankind, are the roots of war. And, like Humpty Dumpty, who could not be put together again, all the efforts of religious leaders, scientists, politicians, and peacemakers will not put our world together in harmony.

The only answer for peace is the salvation found in Christ, foretold by the angels. This is first peace with God: "Therefore being justified by faith, we have peace with God through our Lord Jesus Christ" (Romans 5:1), then peace toward others as God, in the believer, overcomes greed and hate.

The world peace that mankind talks about will be evident the next time Christ comes to earth, to reign for 1000 years: "In the last days the mountain of the LORD's temple will be established as chief among the mountains... He will teach us his ways, so that we may walk in his paths." The law will go out from Zion, the word of the LORD from Jerusalem. He will judge between the nations and will settle disputes for many peoples. They will beat their swords into ploughshares and their spears into pruning hooks. Nation will not take up sword against nation, nor will they train for war any more" (Isaiah 2:2,4 NIV).

"Lest we forget", our present task is to let God, through salvation, rule in our own hearts: "But the wisdom that comes from heaven is first of all pure; then peace-loving, considerate, submissive, full of mercy and good fruit, impartial and sincere" (James 3 NIV).

> Calm soul of all things! make it mine,
> To feel, amid the city's jar,
> That there abides a peace of thine
> Man did not make, and cannot mar!
> The will to neither strive nor cry,
> The power to feel with others give!
> Calm, calm me more! nor let me die,
> Before I have begun to live.
>
> Matthew Arnold (1822-1888)

Personal Notes:

November 15
Psalm 17:1-10

The LORD is my light and my salvation; Whom shall I fear? The LORD is the strength of my life; Of whom shall I be afraid? When the wicked came against me To eat up my flesh, My enemies and foes, They stumbled and fell. Though an army may encamp against me, My heart shall not fear; Though war should rise against me, In this I will be confident. One thing I have desired of the LORD, That will I seek: That I may dwell in the house of the LORD All the days of my life, To behold the beauty of the LORD, And to inquire in His temple. For in the time of trouble He shall hide me in His pavilion; In the secret place of His tabernacle He shall hide me; He shall set me high upon a rock. And now my head shall be lifted up above my enemies all around me; Therefore I will offer sacrifices of joy in His tabernacle; I will sing, yes, I will sing praises to the LORD. Hear, O LORD, when I cry with my voice! Have mercy also upon me, and answer me. When You said, "Seek My face," My heart said to You, "Your face, LORD, I will seek." Do not hide Your face from me; Do not turn your servant away in anger; You have been my help; Do not leave me nor forsake me, O God of my salvation. When my father and my mother forsake me, Then the LORD will take care of me.

Fear of Failure

The hardest thing many people do each day is get up and stare into the mirror first thing in the morning. Although there is some truth to the saying, "beauty is only skin deep", (and skin does tend to get a little wrinkled in the night), the difficulty does not rest in the shock of our physical appearance. The difficulty rests in the deep seated fear carried by many that "to look in the mirror is to face someone who will not measure up." This is the fear that sometime in the day ahead, their inadequacies will surface and the world will laugh mockingly at their failure.

One of the leading causes of depression is this complete lack of personal confidence which leads to a consuming fear of failure. This human malady may be the result of a success driven society, or the consequences of a loveless childhood, or even the memory of past failure. Whatever the reason, the reality of such fear and depression is as certain as sunrise for many.

David may have had similar thoughts as he contemplated life. However, he soon broke free of any depression as he focused on the wonder of man's created place: "...what is man that you are mindful of him, the son of man that you care for him? You made him ruler over the works of your hands; you put everything under his feet: all flocks and herds, and the beasts of the field, the birds of the air, and the fish of the sea, all that swim the paths of the seas" (Psalms 8:3-8 NIV).

David's relation to the Lord was akin to the Christian's. In a similar fashion, finding new life in Christ rekindles a sense of uniqueness. "Therefore, if anyone is in Christ, he is a new creation; the old has gone, the new has come!" (2 Corinthians 5:17 NIV), "How great is the love the Father has lavished on us, that we should be called children of God! And that is what we are!" (1 John 3:1 NIV).

One of the richest blessings of salvation in Christ is the potential for a new outlook on life. Instead of worry over inadequacies and failure, there is afforded to the believer an assurance of unquestioned forgiveness (1 John 1:9), unconditional acceptance (Romans 8:35-39), unlimited strength (Philippians 4:13), undeniable help (Hebrews 4:16), and the unbreakable presence of God (Hebrews 13:5).

This new outlook brings a further liberty. Paul puts this into proper perspective: "Each one should test his own actions. Then he can take pride in himself, without comparing himself to somebody else," (Galatians 6:4 NIV). Because life's focus is toward the Lord who loves us unconditionally, value judgement is between God and self alone. Fear is replaced with faith; despair is overcome by God's love.

Truly, the Christian can stare boldly into the mirror and say: "The LORD is my light and my salvation--whom shall I fear? The LORD is the stronghold of my life--of whom shall I be afraid?" (Psalm 27:1 NIV).

Personal Notes:

November 16
2 Peter 1:1-11

Simon Peter, a bondservant and apostle of Jesus Christ, To those who have obtained like precious faith with us by the righteousness of our God and Saviour Jesus Christ: Grace and peace be multiplied to you in the knowledge of God and of Jesus our Lord, as His divine power has given to us all things that pertain to life and godliness, through the knowledge of Him who called us by glory and virtue, by which have been given to us exceedingly great and precious promises, that through these you may be partakers of the divine nature, having escaped the corruption that is in the world through lust. But also for this very reason, giving all diligence, add to your faith virtue, to virtue knowledge, to knowledge self-control, to self-control perseverance, to perseverance godliness, to godliness brotherly kindness, and to brotherly kindness love. For if these things are yours and abound, you will be neither barren nor unfruitful in the knowledge of our Lord Jesus Christ. For he who lacks these things is short-sighted, even to blindness, and has forgotten that he was cleansed from his old sins. Therefore, brethren, be even more diligent to make your call and election sure, for if you do these things you will never stumble; for so an entrance will be supplied to you abundantly into the everlasting kingdom of our Lord and Saviour Jesus Christ.

Diligence

"Spoudazo" is a Greek word having its root meaning in the era of war where a quick military manoeuvre, such as the urgency of building a wall of defence, was a matter of survival. The word, translated "diligent" or "endeavour" in English, came to mean a labour undertaken with a sense of urgency, a zealous effort requiring total commitment.

God uses this Word in scripture as an expression of that which marks Christian ethics and behaviour. Those who have a personal trust in Christ as Saviour are given five specific things about which to be diligent. There is a need to be diligent about the Christian's Unity in the Spirit. "With all lowliness and meekness, with longsuffering, forbearing one another in love; Endeavouring (being diligent) to keep the unity of the Spirit in the bond of peace" (Ephesians 4:2-3). As the text indicates, this is accomplished with a determination to embrace a humble and servant attitude.

Christians are urged to be diligent regarding their Quality of Workmanship: "Study (be diligent) to show yourself approved unto God, a workman that does not need to be ashamed, rightly dividing the word of truth." (2 Timothy 2:15) Here, the necessity of careful interpretation and application of God's word is the issue. As a tentmaker carefully cuts skins for making tents, so believers are to carefully divide the Word of Truth.

God exhorts the Christian to be diligent about Victory over ungodly life styles that are outside of the Christian ethic and contrary to the true rest found in salvation: "Let us labour (be diligent) therefore to enter into that rest, lest any man fall after the same example of unbelief." (Hebrews 4:11) Believers are similarly called to: "give diligence to make your calling and election sure: for if ye do these things, ye shall never fall" (2 Peter 1:10), where the continued evaluation of life's character changes through the power of God, demonstrate the genuineness of new life in Christ.

Finally, the Christian is urged to be diligent about Purity of Life: "Wherefore, beloved, seeing that ye look for such things, be diligent that ye may be found of him in peace, without spot, and blameless." (2 Peter 3:14) In this text, the individual believer is to be motivated to continued purity of mind and deed by the possibility of the Lord's return, which could take place at any moment, and a desire to be found pleasing Him!

Being reminded of the words of Paul to the Ephesians: "For we wrestle not against flesh and blood, but against principalities, against powers, against the rulers of the darkness of this world, against spiritual wickedness in high places" (Ephesians 6:12). It is easy to see why "spoudazo", that zealous effort requiring total commitment is a part of the Christian's daily warfare with the world, the flesh and the devil, that victory is dependant upon. Christian reader, are you "diligent" about your spiritual duty?

Personal Notes:

November 17
1 John 4:7-16

Beloved, let us love one another, for love is of God; and everyone who loves is born of God and knows God. He who does not love does not know God, for God is love. In this the love of God was manifested toward us, that God has sent His only begotten Son into the world, that we might live through Him. In this is love, not that we loved God, but that He loved us and sent His Son to be the propitiation for our sins. Beloved, if God so loved us, we also ought to love one another. No one has seen God at any time. If we love one another, God abides in us, and His love has been perfected in us. By this we know that we abide in Him, and He in us, because He has given us of His Spirit. And we have seen and testify that the Father has sent the Son as Savior of the world. Whoever confesses that Jesus is the Son of God, God abides in him, and he in God. And we have known and believed the love that God has for us. God is love, and he who abides in love abides in God, and God in him.

An Oasis of Love

Like the Canadian "snowbirds" who head south to avoid the cold harsh winter, so many people seek to find an escape from the cold harsh realities of life. Some seek such escape by abandoning responsibilities or relationships while others look for escape in drugs or alcohol. Still others would find no recourse but denial which results in mental, physical and emotional breakdown.

These avenues of escape do not work. What people really need is the warmth of the love of the Son of God to shine on their lives. The scriptures define God as the source of true love: "...God is love... We love him, because he first loved us" (1 John 4:8,19). 1 Corinthians 13 defines love, therefore the text also details the character of God: "Love (God) is patient, love (God) is kind. It (He) does not envy, it (He) does not boast, it (He) is not proud. It (He) is not rude, it (He) is not self-seeking, it (He) is not easily angered, it (He) keeps no record of wrongs. Love (God) does not delight in evil but rejoices with the truth. It (He) always protects, always trusts, always hopes, always perseveres. Love (God) never fails" (1 Corinthians 13:4-8 NIV).

Notice the oasis of peace found in God - He keeps no record of wrongs. Because Christ in love took upon himself the penalty of man's sin in His death on the cross, all who put their trust in him have the privilege of forgiveness. Peace reigns instead of guilt: "Therefore being justified by faith, we have peace with God through our Lord Jesus Christ" (Romans 5:1).

In God there is an oasis of security, "(He) always protects". David declared the wonder of that promise long before God's Son became man: "The angel of the LORD encampeth round about them that fear him, and delivereth them." (Psalms 34:7) Paul repeated the truth in the New Testament: "...in all these things we are more than conquerors through him that loved us" (Romans 8:37).

Indeed, because God is love, He never fails. His grace is sufficient for any trial or hardship (2 Corinthians 12:9). His promises never fail (Isaiah 40:8). He will never leave his own nor forsake his own (Hebrews 14:5). Even when we fail Him, God awaits our reconciliation and welcomes our return to the fellowship of His love: "If we confess our sins, he is faithful and just to forgive us [our] sins, and to cleanse us from all unrighteousness" (1 John 1:9).

Is the cold harsh reality of life dragging you into despair? Are you longing for some escape? Turn to The Son and be warmed by the oasis of His love. His invitation stands: "Come to me, all you who are weary and burdened, and I will give you rest" (Matthew 11:28 NIV).

Personal Notes:

November 18

1 John 1:1-7

That which was from the beginning, which we have heard, which we have seen with our eyes, which we have looked upon, and our hands have handled, concerning the Word of life— the life was manifested, and we have seen, and bear witness, and declare to you that eternal life which was with the Father and was manifested to us— that which we have seen and heard we declare to you, that you also may have fellowship with us; and truly our fellowship is with the Father and with His Son Jesus Christ. And these things we write to you that your joy may be full. This is the message which we have heard from Him and declare to you, that God is light and in Him is no darkness at all. If we say that we have fellowship with Him, and walk in darkness, we lie and do not practice the truth. But if we walk in the light as He is in the light, we have fellowship with one another, and the blood of Jesus Christ His Son cleanses us from all sin.

Jesus the Son of God

To many people Jesus is only the memory of a flannel graph figure from Sunday School. That Jesus was nicely tucked away in the recesses of the mind, to be hauled out at a needful hour such as sickness or suffering. How different the Jesus of the Bible is: "God...in these last days he has spoken to us by his Son, whom he appointed heir of all things, and through whom he made the universe. The Son is the radiance of God's glory and the exact representation of his being, sustaining all things by his powerful word" (Hebrews 1:1-3).

In this text three characteristics of Jesus, the Son of God, are evident. First, as the "radiance of God's glory", Jesus possesses all the glory of God's perfection. When the Son of God became man through the miraculous conception and virgin birth, "all the fullness of the Godhead" dwelt in Him bodily (Colossians 2:9). Though His glory was not evident as radiant light, the majesty of His perfection was evident in His wonder (his enemies tried numerous times to take him, but Jesus just walked through their midst), in His wisdom (he taught with authority as no man taught before), and in His wrath (twice he cast out the money changers from the temple).

Secondly, as the "exact representation" of God's being, Jesus possessed all the personality of God. Even as God is defined as "light" (1 John 1:5), and "love", so it is true of Jesus. "And the Word was made flesh, and dwelt among us, and we beheld his glory, the glory as of the only begotten of the Father, full of grace and truth." (John 1:14). Jesus was truth and love in the flesh. He graced this earth with the very attributes of God. John marvelled at his own encounter with God's Son: "That which was from the beginning, which we have heard, which we have seen with our eyes, which we have looked at and our hands have touched--this we proclaim concerning the Word of life."(1 John 1:1 NIV).

Finally, the text describes Jesus as the one "sustaining" the whole of creation. As the constant of God's creation, Jesus is that scientifically unexplained force that holds the universe in place, gives mass its gravitational pull, balances the planets and the stars in their orbits and grants man his next breath.

Jesus is no one dimensional flannel graph figure, He is the Son of God. Charles Spurgeon explained this great truth well when he said: "Deity is not to be explained, but to be adored; and the Sonship of Christ is to be accepted as a truth of revelation, to be apprehended by faith, though it cannot be comprehended by understanding. Suffice it for us to say that, in the most appropriate language of the Nicene Creed, Christ is "God of God, Light of Light, very God of very God." Therefore, as the hymn cries out "O, come let us adore Him, Christ the Lord!"

Personal Notes:

November 19
Esther 4:6-17

So Hathach went out to Mordecai in the city square that was in front of the king's gate. And Mordecai told him all that had happened to him, and the sum of money that Haman had promised to pay into the king's treasuries to destroy the Jews. He also gave him a copy of the written decree for their destruction, which was given at Shushan, that he might show it to Esther and explain it to her, and that he might command her to go in to the king to make supplication to him and plead before him for her people. So Hathach returned and told Esther the words of Mordecai. Then Esther spoke to Hathach, and gave him a command for Mordecai: "All the king's servants and the people of the king's provinces know that any man or woman who goes into the inner court to the king, who has not been called, he has but one law: put all to death, except the one to whom the king holds out the golden scepter, that he may live. Yet I myself have not been called to go in to the king these thirty days." So they told Mordecai Esther's words. And Mordecai told them to answer Esther: "Do not think in your heart that you will escape in the king's palace any more than all the other Jews. "For if you remain completely silent at this time, relief and deliverance will arise for the Jews from another place, but you and your father's house will perish. Yet who knows whether you have come to the kingdom for such a time as this?" Then Esther told them to reply to Mordecai: "Go, gather all the Jews who are present in Shushan, and fast for me; neither eat nor drink for three days, night or day. My maids and I will fast likewise. And so I will go to the king, which is against the law; and if I perish, I perish!" So Mordecai went his way and did according to all that Esther commanded him.

Life's Opportunities

Queen Esther was faced with that proverbial position of being between a rock and a hard place. A royal decree had been issued to destroy all her own Jewish people throughout the land of Persia (a territory extending from modern day India to Italy). Yet the law forbade her to approach the king in court to plea for her people as her uncle Mordecai urged. Mordecai challenged her with these words: "For if thou altogether holdest thy peace at this time, then shall there enlargement and deliverance arise to the Jews from another place; but thou and thy father's house shall be destroyed: and who knoweth whether thou art come to the kingdom for such a time as this?" (Esther 4:14).

Three steps of faith privileged Esther to experience God's sovereign work in these dire straights. She pursued the passion of humility. "I also and my maidens will fast likewise" (4:16a). She accepted the place of vulnerability. "and so will I go in unto the king... and if I perish, I perish" (Esther 4:16b). Finally, Esther took the path of opportunity and presented herself to the king, who in turn extended the sceptre which led to the ultimate deliverance of the Jewish people.

Like Esther, every child of God has been given the choice to make life count for God. Those who have accepted Christ as Saviour, who know God's forgiveness and have received the gift of eternal life by faith, have a privilege and a responsibility to rise to. Paul attested to this when he said: "For we are his workmanship, created in Christ Jesus unto good works, which God hath before ordained that we should walk in them" (Ephesians 2:10).

Nevertheless, too many believers, although so equipped by God, turn from His strength and purpose and let opportunity to glorify the Lord slip by. Peter Marshall describes 20th century Christians in these words: "They are like deep-sea divers encased in suits designed for many fathoms deep, marching bravely forth to pull plugs out of bathtubs."

It has been said that opportunity only knocks once, yet in the Christian life, opportunity knocks so often that its knuckles are raw! Christian friend, have you considered these challenging words: "who knoweth whether thou art come to... this family, this church, this job, this community, this circumstance... for such a time as this?" May I urge you to follow the steps of Esther; pursue the path of humility through daily prayer and surrender to God, accept the place of vulnerability - threat of lost position, lost friendship, lost comfort zone, and take the path of opportunity to Glorify God with a word of testimony of His loving grace and His tender care. In doing so you too will see the might hand of God at work and rejoice in His plan for your life. Let your life count for God each day.

Personal Notes:

November 20
Psalm 100:1-5

A Psalm of Thanksgiving: Make a joyful shout to the LORD, all you lands! Serve the LORD with gladness; Come before His presence with singing. Know that the LORD, He is God; It is He who has made us, and not we ourselves; We are His people and the sheep of His pasture. Enter into His gates with thanksgiving, And into His courts with praise. Be thankful to Him, and bless His name. For the LORD is good; His mercy is everlasting, And His truth endures to all generations.

The Potential of Thanksgiving

Rudyard Kipling at one time was so popular that his writings were getting ten shillings per word. A few college students, however, didn't appreciate Kipling's writings; they sarcastically sent him a letter enclosing ten shillings. It read, "Please, send us your best word." They got back a letter from Kipling, "Thanks."

Whether by wit or by sincerity, to suggest that "thanks" is the best word Kipling has provoked some worthwhile thought. Is there another single word among men that can accomplish so much by the power of change? 'Thanks' can change a frown into a smile, a hot temper to a mild manner, a hurt heart into a healed heart. 'Thanks' can change a dark cloud into a bright day, a wasted effort into an enthusiastic attempt, and a low self esteem into an aspiring prodigy.

If one word has so much power of change among men, imagine what thanksgiving can accomplish toward God, especially because it harmonizes with His own will: "Rejoice evermore. Pray without ceasing. In every thing give thanks: for this is the will of God in Christ Jesus concerning you" (1 Thessalonians 5:16-18). It is altogether too sad that in this abundantly blessed country of ours, we Canadians have forgotten the power of change that transpires among people who choose out of grateful hearts, to give thanks to the living God.

Although out of concern for another nation, President Abraham Lincoln's "Proclamation for a National Day of Fasting, Humiliation and Prayer", delivered on April 30, 1863, is a fitting call to all nations on this.

"We have been the recipients of the choicest bounties of heaven. We have been preserved, the many years, in peace and prosperity. We have grown in numbers, wealth and power, as no other nation has ever grown. But we have forgotten God. We have forgotten the gracious hand which preserved us in peace and multiplied and enriched and strengthened us; and we have vainly imagined, in the deceitfulness of our hearts that all these blessings were produced by some superior wisdom and virtue of our own.

Intoxicated with unbroken success, we have become too self-sufficient to feel the necessity of redeeming and preserving grace, too proud to pray to God that made us! It behoves us then, to humble ourselves before the offended Power, to confess our national sins, and to pray for clemency and forgiveness."

Ingratitude is sin. Thanksgiving to God is a privilege, a responsibility, and an avenue of unique change. May this U.S. Thanksgiving holiday include a pointed time of sober thinking and expressed gratitude to God within every family, and may this affect humbled attitudes toward God and helpful actions toward our fellow man.

"O give thanks unto the LORD; call upon his name: make known his deeds among the people. Sing unto him, sing psalms unto him: talk ye of all his wondrous works... Praise ye the LORD. O give thanks unto the LORD; for he is good: for his mercy endures for ever" (Psalms 105:1-2, 106:1).

Personal Notes:

November 21
Psalm 34:1-10

I will bless the LORD at all times: his praise shall continually be in my mouth. My soul shall make her boast in the LORD: the humble shall hear thereof, and be glad. O magnify the LORD with me, and let us exalt his name together. I sought the LORD, and he heard me, and delivered me from all my fears. They looked unto him, and were lightened: and their faces were not ashamed. This poor man cried, and the LORD heard him, and saved him out of all his troubles. The angel of the LORD encampeth round about them that fear him, and delivereth them. O taste and see that the LORD is good: blessed is the man that trusteth in him. O fear the LORD, ye his saints: for there is no want to them that fear him. The young lions do lack, and suffer hunger: but they that seek the LORD shall not want any good thing.

Thanksgiving Every Day

With a beautiful weekend over and Thanksgiving Dinner behind, most homes across our province will face leftovers for the next few days. Do we approach thanksgiving truly being thankful to God, in the same manner - one special day set aside, after which God has to settle with leftover gratefulness?

Thanksgiving is one of the great themes of scripture, clearly evident in Paul's epistles. Paul, writing to the suffering Thessalonians, reminded them that thanksgiving was the very will of God for Christians. He urged: "Rejoice evermore. Pray without ceasing. In every thing give thanks: for this is the will of God in Christ Jesus concerning you" (1 Thessalonians 5).

Writing to the believers at Ephesus, Paul pleaded: "Giving thanks always for all things unto God and the Father in the name of our Lord Jesus Christ" (Ephesians 5:20), and to the Colossians Paul wrote: "And whatsoever ye do in word or deed, do all in the name of the Lord Jesus, giving thanks to God and the Father by him" (Colossians 3:17). Indeed, the New Testament views Thanksgiving as one of the remaining sacrifices to be offered to God: "By him therefore let us offer the sacrifice of praise to God continually, that is, the fruit of our lips giving thanks to his name" (Hebrews 13:15)

It is said that in Africa there is a fruit called the "taste berry", because it changes a person's taste so that everything eaten tastes sweet and pleasant. Sour fruit, even if eaten several hours after the "taste berry," becomes sweet and delicious. Gratitude is the "taste berry" of Christianity, and when our hearts are filled with gratitude, nothing that God sends us seems unpleasant to us.

Thanksgiving should be the normal expression of the believer, in gratitude to God for the gift of salvation and the continued mercy and grace of His care. As one writer put it: "Sorrowing heart, sweeten your grief with gratitude. Burdened soul, lighten your burden by singing God's praises. Disappointed one, dispel your loneliness by making others grateful. Sick one, grow strong in soul, thanking God that He loves you enough to chasten you." Keep the "taste berry" of gratitude in your hearts, and it will do for you what the "taste berry" of Africa does for the African."

Christian friend, don't abandon God to leftover gratefulness, rather, offer the sacrifice of Thanksgiving to Him daily, in prayer, in honour, in tribute, in action, in attitude.

Personal Notes:

November 22
1 John 4:7-10

Beloved, let us love one another, for love is of God; and everyone who loves is born of God and knows God. He who does not love does not know God, for God is love. In this the love of God was manifested toward us, that God has sent His only begotten Son into the world, that we might live through Him. In this is love, not that we loved God, but that He loved us and sent His Son to be the propitiation for our sins.

A Reason for Thankfulness

The crush of circumstances often leaves our heart so full of grief and despair that thanksgiving is far from our mind. How do you give thanks when all the wheels fall off your wagon? At such times the exhortation from scripture: "Rejoice evermore. Pray without ceasing. In every thing give thanks: for this is the will of God in Christ Jesus concerning you" (1 Thessalonians 5:16-18), becomes difficult even for a Christian, when attention is focused on circumstances.

It is especially at such times that the Believer must be reminded of Nehemiah's plea to Israel: "Go your way, eat the fat, and drink the sweet, and send portions unto them for whom nothing is prepared: for this day is holy unto our Lord: neither be ye sorry; for the joy of the LORD is your strength" (Nehemiah 8:10). He spoke these words to Israel after they had heard the Words of Scripture and realized their own sin and waywardness from the living God. The point Nehemiah was making is that, although their sin had resulted in wrong and harmful decisions, God had not abandoned them!

The joy of the Lord that brings thanksgiving is found in one simple yet overwhelming truth; GOD LOVES US! No matter what God's people do, no matter what circumstances they are in, no matter how many wheels fall off their wagon, His people can be assured that God's love will not diminish one "micro bit" toward them.

God assures the Christian of that truth: "Who shall separate us from the love of Christ? Shall trouble or hardship or persecution or famine or nakedness or danger or sword? ... No, in all these things we are more than conquerors through him who loved us. For I am convinced that neither death nor life, neither angels nor demons, neither the present nor the future, nor any powers, neither height nor depth, nor anything else in all creation, will be able to separate us from the love of God that is in Christ Jesus our Lord" (Romans 8 NIV).

    Christian friend, has thanksgiving slipped from you? Here is reason to restore it, in any circumstance: GOD LOVES YOU! Here is a reminder of that love, adopted from a poem by Elizabeth Barrett- Browning:

> HOW does He love me? Let me count the ways.
> He loves me to the depth and breadth and height
> My soul can reach, though feeling out of sight
> Until the ends of time by divine Grace.
> He loves me to the level of everyday's
> Most quiet need, by sun and candle-light.
> He loves me freely, as God alone does strive for Right;
> He loves me purely, even as I turn from Praise.
> He loves me with the passion of the cross
> Bearing my guilt, and granting saving faith.
> He loves me with a love that overcomes all loss
> That with all saints, bestows eternal breath -
> Through smiles and tears of this passing life, and did choose,
> To love me in His presence, after death.

Personal Notes:

November 23
Matthew 17:1-9

Now after six days Jesus took Peter, James, and John his brother, led them up on a high mountain by themselves; and He was transfigured before them. His face shone like the sun, and His clothes became as white as the light. And behold, Moses and Elijah appeared to them, talking with Him. Then Peter answered and said to Jesus, "Lord, it is good for us to be here; if You wish, let us make here three tabernacles: one for You, one for Moses, and one for Elijah." While he was still speaking, behold, a bright cloud overshadowed them; and suddenly a voice came out of the cloud, saying, "This is My beloved Son, in whom I am well pleased. Hear Him!" And when the disciples heard it, they fell on their faces and were greatly afraid. But Jesus came and touched them and said, "Arise, and do not be afraid." When they had lifted up their eyes, they saw no one but Jesus only. Now as they came down from the mountain, Jesus commanded them, saying, "Tell the vision to no one until the Son of Man is risen from the dead."

The Beauty of Change

Time lapse photography is one of the greatest discoveries of modern art and science. To enable a viewer to see a bud blossom into a rose, to watch the marvel of the life cycle of a butterfly transforming from a cocoon to a creature of beauty and grace, can truly be breathtaking. Yet even as these wonders take place around us daily, we often are oblivious to them unless drawn by such modern tools as time lapse photography. Is it possible that the similar wonder of Christian transformation is equally ignored by God's people?

The "time lapse" model for Christian transformation is evident in the life of Christ: "And was transfigured before them: and his face did shine as the sun, and his raiment was white as the light" (Matthew 17:2). Here, before the eyes of the most intimate disciples, the human appearance of Jesus was for a moment changed into that of the heavenly being; God the Son's glory shone forth!

To this end each believer is destined: "Beloved, now are we the sons of God, and it doth not yet appear what we shall be: but we know that, when he shall appear, we shall be like him; for we shall see him as he is" (1 John 3:2). With the hope of such transformation before the Christian, Paul assures the believer that the work has already begun: "But we all, with open face beholding as in a glass the glory of the Lord, are changed into the same image from glory to glory, even as by the Spirit of the Lord" (2 Corinthians 3:18).

Although the process is slow, and is restricted to the believer's inner being: his mind, emotions and will and his moral and ethical character, the work of transformation is a wonder all the same! For this purpose Peter urges the believer to "grow in grace and the knowledge of our Lord and Saviour" (2 Peter 3:18) and Paul reminds the believer of their responsibility in the process: "Therefore, I urge you, brothers, in view of God's mercy, to offer your bodies as living sacrifices, holy and pleasing to God--this is your spiritual act of worship. Do not conform any longer to the pattern of this world, but be transformed by the renewing of your mind" (Romans 12:1-2 NIV). Here Paul calls the Christian to turn away from the world's values and morals, and adopt God's. This is a transformation that begins with a change of thinking (the mind), and progresses to a complete change of heart and soul by the Word of God.

Solomon said: "He (God) has made everything beautiful in its time. He has also set eternity in the hearts of men; yet they cannot fathom what God has done from beginning to end" (Ecclesiastes 3:11 NIV). The transformation of the Christian may not be captured by time lapse photography, but it is a unique work of beauty by our Creator, to be appreciated and responded to in praise every day. Here change is a beautiful thing!

Personal Notes:

November 24
Acts 3:2, 6-9; 4:5-14

And a certain man lame from his mother's womb was carried, whom they laid daily at the gate of the temple which is called Beautiful, to ask alms from those who entered the temple. ... Then Peter said, "Silver and gold I do not have, but what I do have I give you: In the name of Jesus Christ of Nazareth, rise up and walk." And he took him by the right hand and lifted him up, and immediately his feet and ankle bones received strength. So he, leaping up, stood and walked and entered the temple with them—walking, leaping, and praising God. And all the people saw him walking and praising God.

...And it came to pass, on the next day, that their rulers, elders, and scribes, as well as Annas the high priest, Caiaphas, John, and Alexander, and as many as were of the family of the high priest, were gathered together at Jerusalem. And when they had set them in the midst, they asked, "By what power or by what name have you done this?" Then Peter, filled with the Holy Spirit, said to them, "Rulers of the people and elders of Israel: "If we this day are judged for a good deed done to a helpless man, by what means he has been made well, "let it be known to you all, and to all the people of Israel, that by the name of Jesus Christ of Nazareth, whom you crucified, whom God raised from the dead, by Him this man stands here before you whole. "This is the 'stone which was rejected by you builders, which has become the chief cornerstone.' "Nor is there salvation in any other, for there is no other name under heaven given among men by which we must be saved." Now when they saw the boldness of Peter and John, and perceived that they were uneducated and untrained men, they marvelled. And they realized that they had been with Jesus. And seeing the man who had been healed standing with them, they could say nothing against it.

The Only Name

The story is told of a blind man who once stood on a corner at a busy intersection reading aloud Acts 4 from a portion of a Braille Bible. A gentleman on his way home stopped at the edge of the crowd that had gathered to listen. At that very moment, the sightless man lost his place. While trying to find it, he kept repeating the last three words he had just read: "No other name... No other name... No other name..." Many smiled, but the inquisitive bystander went away impressed. He had been searching for inner peace and was ready to be influenced by a few words spoken "in season." He had heard the verse before, but that one phrase haunted him. Before morning he surrendered to the Holy Spirit's wooing and accepted the Saviour. "I see it all now," he cried. "I've been trying to be saved by my own works and prayers. But Jesus alone can help me. He is my mediator. There is no other name whereby I must be saved." Thus a blind man's witness, given in a stumbling manner, was used to lead a seeking soul to Christ.

To quote John MacArthur: "As far as the way of salvation is concerned, there are only two religions the world has ever known or will ever know: the religion of divine accomplishment, which is biblical Christianity, and the religion of human achievement, which includes all other kinds of religion, whatever names they may go under." Either men will seek by their own efforts to be approved before God and forever miss eternal life because "all have sinned, and come short of the glory of God" (Romans 3:23), or men will receive eternal life as God's gift, offered to all who will believe on Christ and by faith turn to Him as the one "who gave himself for us to redeem us from all wickedness and to purify for himself a people that are his very own"(Titus 2:14 NIV).

Salvation, the gift of eternal life, the assurance of forgiveness, a personal relationship with the living God, is only a name and a prayer away: "That if you confess with your mouth, "Jesus is Lord," and believe in your heart that God raised him from the dead, you will be saved. For it is with your heart that you believe and are justified, and it is with your mouth that you confess and are saved" (Romans 10 NIV).

As the blind man read: "Salvation is found in no one else, for there is no other name, NO OTHER NAME, NO OTHER NAME,.. under heaven given to men by which we must be saved" (Acts 4:12 NIV). Dear reader, have you called upon that name?

Personal Notes:

November 25
2 Corinthians 1:3-11

Blessed be the God and Father of our Lord Jesus Christ, the Father of mercies and God of all comfort, who comforts us in all our tribulation, that we may be able to comfort those who are in any trouble, with the comfort with which we ourselves are comforted by God. For as the sufferings of Christ abound in us, so our consolation also abounds through Christ. Now if we are afflicted, it is for your consolation and salvation, which is effective for enduring the same sufferings which we also suffer. Or if we are comforted, it is for your consolation and salvation. And our hope for you is steadfast, because we know that as you are partakers of the sufferings, so also you will partake of the consolation. For we do not want you to be ignorant, brethren, of our trouble which came to us in Asia: that we were burdened beyond measure, above strength, so that we despaired even of life. Yes, we had the sentence of death in ourselves, that we should not trust in ourselves but in God who raises the dead, who delivered us from so great a death, and does deliver us; in whom we trust that He will still deliver us, you also helping together in prayer for us, that thanks may be given by many persons on our behalf for the gift granted to us through many.

Suffering with Contentment

Philip Yancey begins his book "Where is God When it Hurts?" with these words: "I feel hopeless around people in pain. Really, I feel guilty. They lie alone, perhaps moaning, their features twitching, and there is no way I can span the gulf between us to penetrate their suffering. I can only watch. Anything I attempt to say seems weak and stiff, as though I'd memorized the lines for a school play." Suffering is no respecter of persons, it touches the young and the old, the beautiful and the crude, it reaches out without regard to race, creed, language, and inflicts without thought to education, character, wellbeing or potential. The Christian in particular can find consolation in suffering through God's Word. Whether as a tool to help others, or a source of strength for our own suffering, the apostle Paul's example is of great encouragement.

In the Second Epistle of Corinthians, Paul reveals his own view of suffering. It begins with his unique attitude in which he viewed hardship with complete acceptance, understanding that others could claim hardship as well: "Who is weak, and I am not weak? who is offended, and I burn not?" (2 Corinthians 11:28). Paul appears to accept with contentment his suffering as a part of the general suffering all are called to as a result of human frailty.

Yet, he viewed hardship with undeterred hope: "Who delivered us from so great a death, and doth deliver: in whom we trust that he will yet deliver us" (2 Corinthians 1:10). Accepting that the Lord had delivered him from death in the past, he was confident that deliverance was assured again, even if it was the deliverance through death into the presence of God: "We are confident, I say, and willing rather to be absent from the body, and to be present with the Lord." (2 Corinthians 5:8). This hope of glory was indeed preferred by Paul. He was able to project his thoughts into the promised future experience of heaven and, therefore, accept all manner of suffering on the present as a "momentary affliction" (4:17).

Paul viewed hardship as a privilege, affirming that believers are the temple of the living God (6:16), and they are God's own people (6:16). Paul viewed suffering as the privilege of a special commission by God (2:17) as ambassadors for Christ (5:20). The whole emphasis of 6:4-10 focuses on the privilege of being "ministers of God." Paul saw this privilege carrying the believer through every trial with honour.

Therefore, Paul viewed hardship with a purpose. He states that through suffering "the life of Jesus also might be manifested in our body, so then death is working in us, but life in you" (4:11-12). Suffering "for Christ's sake" drew attention to the value of apostolic message. The bold confidence, sure hope and true life in Christ, of Paul and his co-workers, overflowed through hardship, drawing the dying world of Corinth to the living Saviour.

Paul's unique attitude was "Lord, use me anyway you can to point others to Christ!" Christian sufferer, can you say the same?

Personal Notes:

November 26
Psalm 107:1-9

Oh, give thanks to the LORD, for He is good! For His mercy endures forever. Let the redeemed of the LORD say so, Whom He has redeemed from the hand of the enemy, And gathered out of the lands, From the east and from the west, From the north and from the south. They wandered in the wilderness in a desolate way; They found no city to dwell in. Hungry and thirsty, Their soul fainted in them. Then they cried out to the LORD in their trouble, And He delivered them out of their distresses. And He led them forth by the right way, That they might go to a city for a dwelling place. Oh, that men would give thanks to the LORD for His goodness, And for His wonderful works to the children of men! For He satisfies the longing soul, And fills the hungry soul with goodness.

The Wilderness of Want

There is a world of humanity that resides in the desert of want. I do not speak of those wholly without the necessities of life; food, clothing and shelter. Rather, I refer to those who have all these in abundance, yet remain unsatisfied of heart and soul. This segment of humanity is epitomised by the words of the once popular song "I Can't Get No Satisfaction" where attempt after attempt results only in futility. These poor folks find want in virtually every area of life! Although possessing much, these have a deep sense of unfulfilled desire expressing itself in feelings of inferiority, failure, and even fear.

This segment of humanity is described in Psalm 107: "Some wandered in desert wastelands, finding no way to a city where they could settle. They were hungry and thirsty, and their lives ebbed away" (Psalm 107:4-5). It may surprise the reader to know that these were not unbelievers, but were the people of God, as William Jay reminds us: "For the people of God are 'redeemed' [verse 2]: redeemed from the curse of the law, the powers of darkness and the bondage of corruption. They are 'gathered' [verse 3]: gathered by His grace out of all the diversities of the human race; out of all nations and kindreds and peoples and tongues. Whatever this world is to others, they find it to be "a wilderness".

Those who are the children of God (see John 1:12) soon discover that the world's values, entertainment and passions, only bring emptiness, even as Solomon discovered. After his pursuit of wealth and wisdom, pleasure and power, he concluded: "Meaningless! Meaningless!" says the Teacher. "Everything is meaningless!" (Ecclesiastes 12:8 NIV). The Christian who keeps his focus on this world, who seeks success in the world's eyes, who pursues pleasure as the world defines it, wanders in a wilderness of want!

In that wilderness of want, the Believer can learn where true satisfaction is found: "Then they cried out to the LORD in their trouble, and he delivered them from their distress. He led them by a straight way to a city where they could settle. Let them give thanks to the LORD for his unfailing love and his wonderful deeds for men, for he satisfies the thirsty and fills the hungry with good things" (Psalms 107: 6-9 NIV).

The New Testament relates these same truths of emptiness versus fullness: "Do not love the world or anything in the world... everything in the world--the cravings of sinful man, the lust of his eyes and the boasting of what he has and does-- comes not from the Father but from the world. The world and its desires pass away" (1 John 2 NIV). "Come to me, all you who are weary and burdened, and I will give you rest. Take my yoke upon you and learn from me, for I am gentle and humble in heart, and you will find rest for your souls" (Matthew 11:28-29 NIV).

Are you an unsatisfied Christian? Turn your heart fully toward Christ and find an oasis from that wilderness of want.

Personal Notes:

November 27
Psalm 107:10-20

Those who sat in darkness and in the shadow of death, Bound in affliction and irons— Because they rebelled against the words of God, And despised the counsel of the Most High. Therefore, He brought down their heart with labour; They fell down, and there was none to help. Then they cried out to the LORD in their trouble, And He saved them out of their distresses. He brought them out of darkness and the shadow of death, And broke their chains in pieces. Oh, that men would give thanks to the LORD for His goodness, And for His wonderful works to the children of men! For He has broken the gates of bronze, And cut the bars of iron in two. Fools, because of their transgression, And because of their iniquities, were afflicted. Their soul abhorred all manner of food, And they drew near to the gates of death. Then they cried out to the LORD in their trouble, And He saved them out of their distresses. He sent His word and healed them, And delivered them from their destructions.

Setting Prisoners Free

In the Australian bush country grows a little plant called the "sundew." Woe to the insect that dares to dance around it in the sunny air. The shiny moisture on each beautiful leaf is sticky, and will hold any bug prisoner that touches it. The movement of the insect causes the leaves to close tightly. This innocent looking plant actually feeds upon its victims.

Mankind is just as easily entrapped by common vices. Three of these vices are mentioned in Psalm 107. People can be prisoners of spiritual darkness: "Such as sit in darkness and in the shadow of death, being bound in affliction and iron; because they rebelled against the words of God, and contemned the counsel of the most High" (Psalms 107:10-11). Such people reject the authority of God's Word: "The god of this age has blinded the minds of unbelievers, so that they cannot see the light of the gospel of the glory of Christ, who is the image of God" (2 Corinthians 4:4 NIV).

People can become prisoners of wickedness: "Some became fools through their transgression and suffered affliction because of their iniquities. They loathed all food and drew near the gates of death" (Psalms 107:17-18). These are in bondage to the power of desire. Lust consumes their energy, eating life away. James outlines the fatal path of destruction: "But each one is tempted when, by his own evil desire, he is dragged away and enticed. Then, after desire has conceived, it gives birth to sin; and sin, when it is full-grown, gives birth to death" (James 1 NIV).

Fear of death also holds mankind in bondage: "For he spoke and stirred up a tempest that lifted high the waves. They mounted up to the heavens and went down to the depths; in their peril their courage melted away. They reeled and staggered like drunken men; they were at their wits' end" (Psalms 107:25-26 NIV). Hebrews traces the power of fear of death: "... by his [Christ's] death he might destroy him who holds the power of death--that is, the devil-- and free those who all their lives were held in slavery by their fear of death" (Hebrews 2 NIV). Indeed, the fear of death entraps people, placing them in a holding pattern of anxiety, inactivity, and even moment by moment misery.

In each of these situations where men are hopelessly bound, God offers a means of escape. In each case the Psalm states: "Then they cried out to the LORD in their trouble, and he delivered them from their distress" (Psalms 107:6 NIV). In the case of darkness God delivered them from the darkness "and broke their chains in pieces", with regard to wickedness, God "sent His Word and healed them, and delivered them from their destructions." As for fear, God "calms the storm" and "brings them to their desired end".

The reason that Jesus died on the cross was to provide a way for man's deliverance from the bondage of darkness, wickedness and fear. Scripture pleads: "Believe on the Lord Jesus Christ and thou shalt be saved."

Personal Notes:

November 28
Romans 5:1-15

Therefore, having been justified by faith, we have peace with God through our Lord Jesus Christ, through whom also we have access by faith into this grace in which we stand, and rejoice in hope of the glory of God. And not only that, but we also glory in tribulations, knowing that tribulation produces perseverance; and perseverance, character; and character, hope. Now hope does not disappoint, because the love of God has been poured out in our hearts by the Holy Spirit who was given to us. For when we were still without strength, in due time Christ died for the ungodly. For scarcely for a righteous man will one die; yet perhaps for a good man someone would even dare to die. But God demonstrates His own love toward us, in that while we were still sinners, Christ died for us. Much more then, having now been justified by His blood, we shall be saved from wrath through Him. For if when we were enemies we were reconciled to God through the death of His Son, much more, having been reconciled, we shall be saved by His life. And not only that, but we also rejoice in God through our Lord Jesus Christ, through whom we have now received the reconciliation. Therefore, just as through one man sin entered the world, and death through sin, and thus death spread to all men, because all sinned— (For until the law sin was in the world, but sin is not imputed when there is no law. Nevertheless death reigned from Adam to Moses, even over those who had not sinned according to the likeness of the transgression of Adam, who is a type of Him who was to come. But the free gift is not like the offense. For if by the one man's offense many died, much more the grace of God and the gift by the grace of the one Man, Jesus Christ, abounded to many.

Bad News, Good News

Larry Moyer explains: "The Bible contains both BAD NEWS and GOOD NEWS about heaven. Let's look at the bad news first. Romans 3:23 says: "For all have sinned and fall short of the glory of God." To have "sinned" means that we have missed the mark. When we lie, hate, lust, or gossip, we have missed the standard God has set. When the Bible says, "All have sinned and fall short," it mans that we have all come short of God's standard of perfection. In thoughts, words and deeds, we have not been perfect.

But the bad news gets worse. Romans 6:23 says, "For the wages of sin is death." Suppose you worked for one day and got paid $50. That $50 was your wages. That's what you earned. The Bible says that by sinning we have earned death. That means we deserve to die and be separated from God forever. But since there was no way we could come to God, God came to us.

Here's the good news: Christ died for you. Romans 5:8 tells us: "But God demonstrates His own love toward us, in that while we were still sinners, Christ died for us." Suppose you are in a hospital dying of cancer. I come to you and say," Let's take the cancer cells from your body and put them into my body." If that were possible, I would die instead of you. The Bible says Christ took the penalty that we deserved for sin and placed it upon Himself. He died in our place. Three days later Christ came back to life to prove that sin and death had been conquered and that His claims to be God were true.

Just as the bad news got worse, the good news gets better! You can be saved through faith in Christ. Ephesians 2:8,9 says, "For by grace (undeserved favour) you have been saved (delivered from sin's penalty) through faith, and that not of yourselves; it is the gift of God, not of works, that no one anyone should boast." Faith means trust. What must you trust Christ for? You must depend on Him alone to forgive you and to give you eternal life.

Even as you trust a chair to hold you through no effort of your own, so you must trust Jesus Christ to get you to heaven through no effort of your own. But you may say, "I'm religious." "I go to church." "I don't steal." "I'm a good person." "I help the poor." These are all good, but good living cannot get you to heaven. You must trust in Jesus Christ alone, and God will give you eternal life as a gift! Think carefully. There is nothing more important than your need to trust Christ. Why not pray right now and tell God you are trusting in His Son? Remember, it is not a prayer that saves you. It is trusting Jesus Christ that saves you.

Prayer is the statement of that trust.

Personal Notes:

November 29
Luke 19:1-10

Then Jesus entered and passed through Jericho. Now behold, there was a man named Zacchaeus who was a chief tax collector, and he was rich. And he sought to see who Jesus was, but could not because of the crowd, for he was of short stature. So he ran ahead and climbed up into a sycamore tree to see Him, for He was going to pass that way. And when Jesus came to the place, He looked up and saw him, and said to him, "Zacchaeus, make haste and come down, for today I must stay at your house." So he made haste and came down, and received Him joyfully. But when they saw it, they all complained, saying, "He has gone to be a guest with a man who is a sinner." Then Zacchaeus stood and said to the Lord, "Look, Lord, I give half of my goods to the poor; and if I have taken anything from anyone by false accusation, I restore fourfold." And Jesus said to him, "Today salvation has come to this house, because he also is a son of Abraham; "for the Son of Man has come to seek and to save that which was lost."

Life's Greatest Event

"Meeting Jesus is the single most important event of any and every life. The person who has met Christ is complete even if everything else in life goes wrong... even if that person never produces anything else of significance. The person who has not met Him, no matter what else he or she accomplishes, is empty, not just by comparison but, on the scale of eternity, *absolutely* empty." (Source unknown).

How can I say that? Because of whom Jesus is. He is the music to a concert. He is the air to a deep breath. He is the gravity to falling. He is life to living. Try life with Jesus, and then try life without him. You'll see what I mean.""What does it mean to meet Christ? Two things, as I see it. First, meeting Christ is an Event. It is to encounter him: to embrace and be embraced. It is to grasp the basic essence of Jesus and to understand with childlike simplicity what he has done for you and its importance to your life and destiny.

You meet Jesus when you place your trust in him as completely as you know how and, as a result, receive the irrevocable gift of eternal life. It is an Event in which you begin a journey with him determined to stay with him all the way to the end, no matter what."

"Meeting Christ is also a Process. It's the journey itself, the adventure of traveling with him over whatever terrain you encounter. It's the adventure that warms up in time and blasts off in eternity. " (Robert Rasmussen in *Imagine Meeting Him*).

When Zacchaeus met Jesus, it was life transforming: "Then Zacchaeus stood and said to the Lord, "Look, Lord, I give half of my goods to the poor; and if I have taken anything from anyone by false accusation, I restore fourfold." And Jesus said to him, "Today salvation has come to this house, because he also is a son of Abraham; for the Son of Man has come to seek and to save that which was lost." (Luke 19). The invitation to Life's Greatest Event still stands! Jesus said: "Behold, I stand at the door and knock. If anyone hears My voice and opens the door, I will come in to him and dine with him, and he with Me." (Revelation 3:20).

Pusan is one of the lesser sun-gods of Vedic Hinduism. He is the shepherd and protector of flocks, the pathfinder for those on a journey, and is particularly called upon to search for lost objects. What a trivial job for a god, finding the lost objects of daily life! The God of the Bible is not concerned with lost objects, but with lost people! (Robert C. Shannon). Friend, have you met Jesus – has Jesus found you?

Personal Notes:

November 30
John 17:6-17

"I have manifested Your name to the men whom You have given Me out of the world. They were Yours, You gave them to Me, and they have kept Your word. "Now they have known that all things which You have given Me are from You. "For I have given to them the words which You have given Me; and they have received them, and have known surely that I came forth from You; and they have believed that You sent Me. "I pray for them. I do not pray for the world but for those whom You have given Me, for they are Yours. "And all Mine are Yours, and Yours are Mine, and I am glorified in them. "Now I am no longer in the world, but these are in the world, and I come to You. Holy Father, keep through Your name those whom You have given Me, that they may be one as We are. "While I was with them in the world, I kept them in Your name. Those whom You gave Me I have kept; and none of them is lost except the son of perdition, that the Scripture might be fulfilled. "But now I come to You, and these things I speak in the world, that they may have My joy fulfilled in themselves. "I have given them Your word; and the world has hated them because they are not of the world, just as I am not of the world. "I do not pray that You should take them out of the world, but that You should keep them from the evil one. "They are not of the world, just as I am not of the world. "Sanctify them by Your truth. Your word is truth.

What Is Truth?

Perhaps the greatest question ever asked fell from the lips of Pilate as he queried Christ, before the cross. His question, like an airport light-beacon, still circles the shifting space of human values. His question, like a lighthouse beacon still pierces the dense fog of human thought. His question is "What is truth?"

Jesus answered that very question in His prayer recorded in John 17. He prayed for those who would believe in Him, that God would: "Sanctify them by your truth. **Your word is truth.**" Consider what Jesus believed about the Scripture as absolute truth: He believed in the literal interpretation of the Genesis account of creation and that Adam and Eve were two uniquely created individuals, brought together in marriage by God as the first family (Matthew 19:4,5). Jesus believed in a literal interpretation of Noah, the ark and a universal flood (Matthew 24:37-40). He believed in Jonah being swallowed by a fish and spit up three days later (Matthew 12:40, 41).

He believed in the prophecies of Daniel, and called him by name (Matt. 24:15). He believed in the actual supernatural destruction of Sodom and Gomorrah (Luke 17:29) and the turning to salt of Lot's wife (verse 32).

Jesus was so committed to the authority of each word of Old Testament Scripture as God's source of Truth for man that he made this bold declaration: "For assuredly, I say to you, till heaven and earth pass away, one jot or one tittle (the two smallest strokes – a letter and a vowel mark of the Hebrew alphabet) will by no means pass from the law till all is fulfilled." He further stated: "Heaven and earth will pass away, but My words will by no means pass away." (Luke 21:33), and explained how His Word would be passed on to the New Testament writers: "when He, the Spirit of truth, has come, He will guide you into all truth; for He will not speak on His own authority, but whatever He hears He will speak; and He will tell you things to come. "He will glorify Me, for He will take of what is Mine and declare it to you." (John 16:13-14).

Therefore, Jesus endorsed the Old Testament writers as well as the New Testament writers, as giving man God's very Word. Jesus made commitment to the entire Word of Truth (the Bible) a test of freedom from sin and error - John 8:32, a test of discipleship -John 8:31, a test of prayer life - John 15:7, and the standard of future judgement – John 12:48.

As Harold Lindsell once wrote: "Of all the doctrines connected with the Christian faith, none is more important than the one that has to do with the basis of our religious knowledge. For anyone who professes the Christian faith the root question is: "From where do I get my knowledge on which my faith is based?" Lindsell answers the question with a historical fact: "From the historical perspective it can be said that for two thousand years the Christian church has agreed that the Bible is completely trustworthy; it is infallible, inerrant." (*The Battle for the Bible, Zondervan Publishing*). The Jesus of the Bible believed it so, do you?

Personal Notes:

December 1
John 20:26-31

And after eight days His disciples were again inside, and Thomas with them. Jesus came, the doors being shut, and stood in the midst, and said, "Peace to you!" Then He said to Thomas, "Reach your finger here, and look at My hands; and reach your hand here, and put it into My side. Do not be unbelieving, but believing." And Thomas answered and said to Him, "My Lord and my God!" Jesus said to him, "Thomas, because you have seen Me, you have believed. Blessed are those who have not seen and yet have believed." And truly Jesus did many other signs in the presence of His disciples, which are not written in this book; but these are written that you may believe that Jesus is the Christ, the Son of God, and that believing you may have life in His name.

What You Don't Know Can Destroy!

Our medical practitioners are constantly reminding us of the importance of self examination and regular check ups for the purpose of early detection of cancer. However, that word strikes such fear into hearts that many who sense something wrong still refuse to seek professional examination. There seems to be a false belief that what you don't know won't hurt you. The result is the advancement of disease which might have been successfully dealt with. This fear and false belief did not commence with cancer; such careless false belief was faced by another master healer, the Lord Jesus.

As Jesus walked among men, many came to be healed of their diseases. Scripture states not only that the Lord healed many but that there was a reason for the healings: "But that ye may know that the Son of man hath power upon earth to forgive sins, (he said unto the sick of the palsy,) I say unto thee, Arise, and take up thy couch, and go into thine house." (Luke 5:24). The power to miraculously heal (and raise the dead, and walk on water, and feed the thousands) confirmed the accuracy of the message Jesus declared that through him forgiveness of sins could be found.

Despite the miracles and the message, there were always those who refused self examination for fear of the truth. In this same passage Jesus stated: "And Jesus answering said unto them, They that are whole need not a physician; but they that are sick. I came not to call the righteous, but sinners to repentance." (Luke 5:31-32). The Pharisees of Jesus' day could not bear to face the fact that "all have sinned, and come short of the glory of God;" (Romans 3:23); consequently, they ignored a problem that with repentance and faith could have been dealt with before eternal suffering came. The Bible is clear about that: "For God so loved the world, he gave his only begotten Son, that whosoever believeth in him should not perish, but have everlasting life... He that believeth on him is not condemned: but he that believeth not is condemned already, because he hath not believed in the name of the only begotten Son of God. (John 3:16, 18).

"The Lord ... is longsuffering to us-ward, not willing that any should perish, but that all should come to repentance." (2 Peter 3:9). For this reason, even as our doctors of medicine plead physical self- examination and professional help, God pleads spiritual self-examination and Christ's help. Sin separates all man from God, and if left unattended, that separation will last through eternity. What you don't know (or more likely refuse to face) will not only hurt, but cause suffering forever. The master healer still pleads: "Verily, verily, I say unto you, He that heareth my word, and believeth on him that sent me, hath everlasting life, and shall not come into condemnation; but is passed from death unto life." (John 5:24)

Personal Notes:

December 2
Hebrews 2:2-9

For if the word spoken through angels proved steadfast, and every transgression and disobedience received a just reward, how shall we escape if we neglect so great a salvation, which at the first began to be spoken by the Lord, and was confirmed to us by those who heard Him, God also bearing witness both with signs and wonders, with various miracles, and gifts of the Holy Spirit, according to His own will? For He has not put the world to come, of which we speak, in subjection to angels. But one testified in a certain place, saying: "What is man that You are mindful of him, Or the son of man that You take care of him? You have made him a little lower than the angels; You have crowned him with glory and honour, And set him over the works of Your hands. You have put all things in subjection under his feet." For in that He put all in subjection under him, He left nothing that is not put under him. But now we do not yet see all things put under him. But we see Jesus, who was made a little lower than the angels, for the suffering of death crowned with glory and honour, that He, by the grace of God, might taste death for everyone.

Christmas Visitation

For most families the Christmas season involves not only the busy schedule of shopping for gifts but the careful planning of visits to all those family members and friends that mean so much to us. How interesting that both gifts and visitation were a part of that first Christmas. The theme of gift giving at Christmas time is easily related to the first Christmas when God sent his Son into the world as a gift of His love. The Bible also speaks of this coming of Christ as a matter of visitation: "But one in a certain place testified, saying, 'What is man, that thou art mindful of him? or the son of man, that thou visitest him?" (Hebrews 2:6) It is important to realize however that the word here translated visit means far more than dropping in to say hello. This word 'visit' (episkeptomai) means to look upon in order to help. God's gift of love was more than an expression of identity with humanity as God became flesh; it was the action of a loving God in dealing with man's problem of sin. God helped man by doing what man could not do himself, that is, pay the penalty of sin through the sacrificial death of Jesus. Scripture boldly declares:

"But God commendeth his love toward us, in that, while we were yet sinners, Christ died for us." (Romans 5:8).

As much as the real meaning of Christmas Visitation is incomplete without the Cross of Easter, so is the Christian life (which begins by appropriating the finished work of the cross through faith - Ephesians 2:8) incomplete without visitation. James stated this truth this way: "this pure and undefiled religion in the sight of God our Father, to visit orphans and widows in their distress, and to keep oneself unstained by the world." (James 1:27) Visitation in the same sense of "looking upon to help" is part of what defines the Christian life. True saving faith results in the inward change of heart that drives a believer to deny self for the benefit and spiritual welfare of others. The transforming power of the gospel manifests itself in the believer's social and personal ethics. Here is seen as "Sympathy with suffering" and "separation from sin".

As the rush of gift buying and visit planning rushes upon us this year, may I encourage each reader to take a moment and reflect upon the real "Visitation of Christmas". Has the Son of God "visited" you personally in dealing with sin? Is your faith in the cross where Christ met that need through His death? Having come to know Christ as Saviour, are you involved in true visitation? Why not take time this season and truly "visit" by helping a family in need through contributing to a food bank, serving at a soup kitchen, or by some other meaningful expression of sacrifice to demonstrate your life changing faith? Wouldn't the world be a different place if every confessing Christian made the Christmas themes of gifts and visitation a year-round expression of their original meaning?

Personal Notes:

December 3
Isaiah 42:1-12

"Behold! My Servant whom I uphold, My Elect One in whom My soul delights! I have put My Spirit upon Him; He will bring forth justice to the Gentiles. He will not cry out, nor raise His voice, Nor cause His voice to be heard in the street. A bruised reed He will not break, And smoking flax He will not quench; He will bring forth justice for truth. He will not fail nor be discouraged, Till He has established justice in the earth; And the coastlands shall wait for His law."

Thus says God the LORD, Who created the heavens and stretched them out, Who spread forth the earth and that which comes from it, Who gives breath to the people on it, And spirit to those who walk on it: "I, the LORD, have called You in righteousness, And will hold Your hand; I will keep You and give You as a covenant to the people, As a light to the Gentiles, To open blind eyes, To bring out prisoners from the prison, Those who sit in darkness from the prison house. I am the LORD, that is My name; And My glory I will not give to another, Nor My praise to carved images. Behold, the former things have come to pass, And new things I declare; Before they spring forth I tell you of them."

Sing to the LORD a new song, And His praise from the ends of the earth, You who go down to the sea, and all that is in it, You coastlands and you inhabitants of them! Let the wilderness and its cities lift up their voice, The villages that Kedar inhabits. Let the inhabitants of Sela sing, Let them shout from the top of the mountains. Let them give glory to the LORD, And declare His praise in the coastlands.

The Real Spirit of the Season

It might be beneficial, as the Christmas season rushes at us, and before we are overcome by the chaos of activity, to take a look at the real "spirit of Christmas" as expressed in God's Word: "Your attitude should be the same as that of Christ Jesus: Who, being in very nature God, did not consider equality with God something to be grasped, but made himself nothing, taking the very nature of a servant, being made in human likeness." (Philippians 2:5-7 NIV).

Although the manger scene is foremost in our minds, the wonder of the Christmas story is the incarnation; God becoming man. Paul reminds us in the Philippians passage that God, in the incarnation, denied himself. God the Son gave up what was rightfully His. As eternal, triune God, the Son possesses full equality with The Father and The Holy Spirit, yet in the incarnation He denied Himself that sovereign position. He did not cling to the honour and the glory of His rightful position, an honour and glory that the angels fall on their faces before, and all creation will one day bow to. Instead, His appearance among mankind was as any child. Although the world has never brought forth such royalty, nor conceived such majesty, this God-child was born in the humble surroundings of a barn.

Paul tells us that this denial was one of complete emptying by the "taking the form of a servant". Jesus the God-man did not become less than God in the incarnation. The word "taking" emphasises an addition not an exchange. Jesus was not emptied of the form of God, but in becoming man, He was emptied of the manner of existence as God, when He took on humanity. Similar to Mark Twain's prince in "The Prince and the Pauper", God the Son set aside the insignia of majesty, while retaining full royalty (deity). While on earth, Jesus chose to operate in the will and power of The Father and The Spirit, laying aside independent use of His divine attributes. This true spirit of Christmas, a selfless surrender to the Will of God, was evident in the life of Christ from the humble manger birth to the cross where Jesus bore the agony of the world's sins.

In a world of selfishness and self-centredness, where comfort takes precedence over commitment, and convenience often rules over care, a reminder of the true spirit of Christmas is certainly needed. Before the rush is fully upon us, take time to reread the Christmas story (Matthew 1:18-2:23, Luke 1:26-2:20). As you read the texts, remember who it is that entered into human history in such a humble fashion; Jesus, the Christ, the Son of God. Remember that this expression of humility and emptying was on your behalf: "And being found in appearance as a man, he humbled himself and became obedient to death--even death on a cross!" (Philippians 2:8 NIV), then pursue the true spirit of Christmas in selfless surrender to God.

Personal Notes:

December 4
Ecclesiastes 12:6-14

Remember your Creator before the silver cord is loosed, Or the golden bowl is broken, Or the pitcher shattered at the fountain, Or the wheel broken at the well. Then the dust will return to the earth as it was, And the spirit will return to God who gave it.
"Vanity of vanities," says the Preacher, "All is vanity." And moreover, because the Preacher was wise, he still taught the people knowledge; yes, he pondered and sought out and set in order many proverbs. The Preacher sought to find acceptable words; and what was written was upright—words of truth. The words of the wise are like goads, and the words of scholars are like well-driven nails, given by one Shepherd. And further, my son, be admonished by these. Of making many books there is no end, and much study is wearisome to the flesh.
Let us hear the conclusion of the whole matter: Fear God and keep His commandments, For this is man's all. For God will bring every work into judgment, Including every secret thing, Whether good or evil.

Life is...

I once read about a man who was so absent-minded that after arriving in New York he phoned his home office and asked; "Why am I here? What am I to do?" Although I would not propose that anyone aspire to such a degree of forgetfulness, answering those questions within ourselves will give us a clear picture of our attitude toward life.

Here are some expressions of attitude toward life. To some life is a dream, "An American dream, life, liberty, and the pursuit of happiness". To others life is a burden; "if life were a bed of roses, some people could never be happy until they developed an allergy". Life, says another "is that period of existence between not knowing anything and not caring any more."

The woman whom Jesus met at the well undoubtedly felt much the same way about life. She was a social outcast due to her moral failures and an "outsider" in the eyes of the Jewish leaders by virtue of her supposed inferior birth as a Samaritan.

In the midst of her poor view of life, Jesus shared this refreshing news: "Everyone who drinks this water will be thirsty again, but whoever drinks the water I give him will never thirst. Indeed, the water I give him will become in him a spring of water welling up to eternal life." (John 4:13-14 NIV). Her acceptance of Jesus as the Christ during the ensuing dialogue proved the truth of His claim. She drank deeply of His truth and gained a completely renewed life in a clear expression of visible repentance: "Many of the Samaritans from that town believed in him because of the woman's testimony, "He told me everything I ever did." (John 4:39 NIV)

In the midst of our society's cynicism the message of this gospel has equally refreshing value. To all who sense an emptiness within, to all who would state with Solomon, "Meaningless, meaningless, everything is meaningless" (Ecclesiastes 1:2), to all who can only find allergies in the midst of roses, Jesus is the answer for a renewed life. Jesus declared, "I am the bread of life. He who comes to me will never go hungry, and he who believes in me will never be thirsty." (John 6:35 NIV)

Richard Blanchard penned this promise in a song: "Like the woman at the well I was seeking, for things that could not satisfy, and then I heard my Saviour speaking, draw from the well that never shall run dry" - Fill my cup Lord, I lift it up Lord! Come and quench this thirsting of my soul; Bread of heaven, feed me till I want no more-Fill my cup, fill it up and make me whole!"

Is life for you all empty dreams and heavy burdens? Let the Lord fill it with His new life.

Personal Notes:

December 5
Isaiah 9:1-7

Nevertheless the gloom will not be upon her who is distressed, As when at first He lightly esteemed The land of Zebulun and the land of Naphtali, And afterward more heavily oppressed her, By the way of the sea, beyond the Jordan, In Galilee of the Gentiles. The people who walked in darkness have seen a great light; Those who dwelt in the land of the shadow of death, Upon them a light has shined. You have multiplied the nation and increased its joy; They rejoice before You According to the joy of harvest, As men rejoice when they divide the spoil. For You have broken the yoke of his burden And the staff of his shoulder, The rod of his oppressor, As in the day of Midian. For every warrior's sandal from the noisy battle, And garments rolled in blood, Will be used for burning and fuel of fire. For unto us a Child is born, Unto us a Son is given; And the government will be upon His shoulder. And His name will be called Wonderful, Counselor, Mighty God, Everlasting Father, Prince of Peace. Of the increase of His government and peace there will be no end, Upon the throne of David and over His kingdom, To order it and establish it with judgment and justice From that time forward, even forever. The zeal of the LORD of hosts will perform this.

More Than Meets the Eye!

Most have read (with a measure of envy) about people finding items of great value in the most unlikely spots; for example, the giant diamond that was purchased for mere pennies at an open market, the rare stamp that was picked up at a garage sale, the original painting purchased at a pawn shop. Although some of these finds are unexpected surprises, they are often the result of a keen eye in recognizing that "there is more than meets the eye".

This holds true regarding the Christmas story as well. For many, the story stops with the cute child in the manger, yet like the diamond in the square, there is more here than meets the eye. Simeon saw with discerning eyes far more than a sweet baby, he said: "my eyes have seen Your salvation, which you have prepared in the sight of all people, a light for revelation to the Gentiles and for glory to your people Israel." (Luke 2:30-32 NIV). Simeon understood that the child was God's provision for the salvation of mankind, the expression of God's loving care. Determined before the foundation of the world, the child was destined to be the Lamb of God that would take away the sin of the world. (see Revelation 13:8)

The wise men, with equally discerning eyes, saw the King of Kings, one worthy of royal gifts and reverent worship: "On coming to the house, they saw the child with his mother Mary, and they bowed down and worshipped him. Then they opened their treasures and presented him with gifts of gold and of incense and of myrrh." (Matthew 2:11 NIV). This child was the sovereign Lord of Glory whose dominion is from everlasting to everlasting, and whose kingdom was prepared from the foundation of the world. (see Matthew 25:34)

With every measurement that makes things uniquely priceless, the babe in the manger surpasses all. In rarity, He is the Only Begotten Son; in age, He is the Beginning and the End, the One from before time; in beauty, He is the lily of the valley, the fairest of ten thousand, the bright and morning star. The child in the manger was the one for whom countless numbers of faithful followers of the living God in ages past looked longingly. And now that He has come, all can look upon the texts of Holy Script and see with discerning eyes, and believing hearts.

Paul realized the importance of discerning vision when he prayed: "asking that the God of our Lord Jesus Christ, the glorious Father, may give you the Spirit of wisdom and revelation, so that you may know him better. I pray also that the eyes of your heart may be enlightened in order that you may know the hope of his calling," (Ephesians 1:17-18).

There is great value in the Christmas message, eternal value worthy of more than a passing seasonal glance. Do not let the pricelessness of the Christmas Child pass you by.

Personal Notes:

December 6

Jeremiah 17:5-11

Thus says the LORD: "Cursed is the man who trusts in man and makes flesh his strength, Whose heart departs from the LORD. For he shall be like a shrub in the desert, And shall not see when good comes, But shall inhabit the parched places in the wilderness, In a salt land which is not inhabited. "Blessed is the man who trusts in the LORD, And whose hope is the LORD. For he shall be like a tree planted by the waters, Which spreads out its roots by the river, And will not fear when heat comes; But its leaf will be green, And will not be anxious in the year of drought, Nor will cease from yielding fruit. "The heart is deceitful above all things, And desperately wicked; Who can know it? I, the LORD, search the heart, I test the mind, Even to give every man according to his ways, According to the fruit of his doings. "As a partridge that broods but does not hatch, So is he who gets riches, but not by right; It will leave him in the midst of his days, And at his end he will be a fool."

The Scrooge in All.

Ebenezer Scrooge in Charles Dickens' story found genuine happiness and was forever changed, much to the joy of the community. However, for most, the "scrooge in us" usually resurfaces after the Christmas season is over. . In truth, all the good will during "the season to be jolly" fails as the season passes because: "Out of the abundance of the heart the mouth speaks" (Matthew 12:34). As has been often stated, "the heart of the matter is the matter of the heart". An unchanged heart cannot hold on to a changed attitude.

When the angels announced the birth of Jesus with "peace and goodwill toward men", more than an encouraging wish was expressed. They were declaring the will of God the Father who would provide the only means for that peace through the offering of His Son: "He was delivered over to death for our sins and was raised to life for our justification. Therefore, since we have been justified through faith, we have peace with God through our Lord Jesus Christ," (Romans 4:25-5:1 NIV).

This repentance toward God and faith in His Son's death for our sins and subsequent resurrection for our justification, coincides with a changed heart: "Therefore, if anyone is in Christ, he is a new creation; the old has gone, the new has come!" (2 Corinthians 5:17 NIV). John spoke of this new heart as experiencing the fullness of Christ: "And of his fullness have all we received, and grace for grace." (John 1:16)

This fullness is described by Charles Spurgeon: "There is a fullness of blessing unspeakable, unknown; a fullness at all times; a fullness by day and a fullness by night; a fullness of comfort in affliction, a fullness of guidance in prosperity, a fullness of every divine attribute, of wisdom, of power, of love; a fullness which it were impossible to survey, much less to explore."

It is only here that the heart can grasp with permanence the changed attitude of year round "good will to man". Only here is the heart moved with a new fullness. To this end, Charles Dickens' "Christmas Carol" offers a meaningful allegory. As with Ebenezer Scrooge, good will does not come from good intention but as a result of a changed heart experienced through revelation that brings repentance. To mankind, the agents for changed hearts are the revelation of scripture applied by the Holy Ghost. So transforming is this change of heart that the Bible calls it being "born again": "For you have been born again, not of perishable seed, but of imperishable, through the living and enduring word of God" (1 Peter 1:23 NIV).

In Christ there is a permanent "good will" to be found by those who would let the Spirit and the Word touch their hearts with truth. In Christ, every season is a season to be joyful.

Personal Notes:

December 7
Isaiah 55:1-9

"Ho! Everyone who thirsts, Come to the waters; And you who have no money, Come, buy and eat. Yes, come, buy wine and milk without money and without price. Why do you spend money for what is not bread, and your wages for what does not satisfy? Listen carefully to Me, and eat what is good, And let your soul delight itself in abundance. Incline your ear, and come to Me. Hear, and your soul shall live; And I will make an everlasting covenant with you—The sure mercies of David. Indeed I have given him as a witness to the people, a leader and commander for the people. Surely you shall call a nation you do not know, and nations who do not know you shall run to you, Because of the LORD your God, And the Holy One of Israel; For He has glorified you."

Seek the LORD while He may be found, Call upon Him while He is near. Let the wicked forsake his way, And the unrighteous man his thoughts; Let him return to the LORD, and He will have mercy on him; And to our God, For He will abundantly pardon. *"For My thoughts are not your thoughts, nor are your ways My ways,"* says the LORD. *"For as the heavens are higher than the earth, so are My ways higher than your ways, And My thoughts than your thoughts.*

The Perfect Gift

As we approach the Christmas season and rush around from store to store looking for that perfect gift, it might do us all good to take a moment and ask "Why?" The patented answer would of course be "Because Christmas stands for giving", or "We celebrate Christmas by giving because God gave us his Son."

Somewhere in the back of Mr. or Mrs. Average Canadian is a basic understanding of the starting place of Christmas. However, in reducing the season to a celebration of exchanged good will and gifts misses the intent of God in sending His Son. I'm reminded of what the Old Testament prophet said: "Why do you spend money for what is not bread? and your wages for what does not satisfy? Listen diligently to me, and eat what is good, and let your soul delight itself in abundance." (Isaiah 55:2)

Much like our approach to Christmas, Israel was going through a form of religious and national tradition that left them empty when completed. Although sharing and celebrating were enjoyable experiences, their souls remained dry and their lives spiritually parched.

God sent His Son to remove the parched condition by providing a means for man to regain a fulfilling relationship with the living God. Isaiah cried: "Ho! Everyone who thirsts, come to the waters: and you who have no money, come buy and eat. Yes, come, buy wine and milk without money and without price" (Isaiah 55:1 NKJ). Christ said: "I am the bread of life. He who comes to me will never go hungry, and he who believes in me will never be thirsty" (John 6:35 NIV).

With your present approach to the season, when Christmas is over, what will be the condition of your soul? Will the season's festivities gloss over the real heart condition only to return to a dry and thirsty life? If so, then the whole purpose of Christmas has been missed.

Why not decide now to change direction, to receive God's perfect gift to mankind - eternal life in His Son: "For God so loved the world that he gave his one and only Son, that whoever believes in him shall not perish but have eternal life" (John 3:16 NIV).

Christmas is about satisfying emptiness: "... the angel said to them, "Do not be afraid. I bring you good news of great joy that will be for all the people. Today in the town of David a Saviour has been born to you; he is Christ the Lord" (Luke 2:10-11 NIV).

Personal Notes:

December 8
Matthew 5:2-16

Then He opened His mouth and taught them, saying: "Blessed are the poor in spirit, for theirs is the kingdom of heaven. Blessed are those who mourn, for they shall be comforted. Blessed are the meek, for they shall inherit the earth. Blessed are those who hunger and thirst for righteousness, for they shall be filled. Blessed are the merciful, for they shall obtain mercy. Blessed are the pure in heart, for they shall see God. Blessed are the peacemakers, for they shall be called sons of God. Blessed are those who are persecuted for righteousness' sake, for theirs is the kingdom of heaven. "Blessed are you when they revile and persecute you, and say all kinds of evil against you falsely for My sake. "Rejoice and be exceedingly glad, for great is your reward in heaven, for so they persecuted the prophets who were before you. "You are the salt of the earth; but if the salt loses its flavour, how shall it be seasoned? It is then good for nothing but to be thrown out and trampled underfoot by men. "You are the light of the world. A city that is set on a hill cannot be hidden. "Nor do they light a lamp and put it under a basket, but on a lampstand, and it gives light to all who are in the house. "Let your light so shine before men, that they may see your good works and glorify your Father in heaven."

Thunder & Lightning

Mark Twain once wrote: "Thunder is good and thunder is impressive, but it is lightning that does the work." Undoubtedly Christianity has its parallel. The "big noise" of those who claim Christianity has little effect on the world, it is the light seen in a life that carries the impact. To all believers, Christ said: "Let your light so shine before men, that they may see your good works, and glorify your Father which is in heaven." (Matthew 5:16).

This theme of light is evident throughout scripture and presents a meaningful responsibility to every Christian. The Bible states that "God is light" (1 John 1:5). Light is one of the transitive attributes of God. Man can only begin to understand this in terms of God's perfection and purity, where no darkness or corruption can exist, the glory of God's being is evident as delicate, pure, brilliant light.

The Bible itself is defined as light: "Thy word [is] a lamp unto my feet, and a light unto my path." (Psalms 119:105) Jesus qualified this by the words of His prayer in John 17 where He stated: "Thy Word is Truth". As absolute truth, given by God through the empowerment and leading of the Holy Spirit, scripture, like God, is without error and therefore "useful for teaching, rebuking, correcting and training in righteousness," (2 Timothy 3:16 NIV).

Jesus is described as the light of the world: "In Him was life; and the life was the light of men." (John 1:4). It is Christ who brought the reality of God's righteousness to man and supplied the sacrifice for sin. It is Christ who provides the way to God through the cross: "But God commendeth his love toward us, in that, while we were yet sinners, Christ died for us. Much more then, being now justified by his blood, we shall be saved from wrath through him." (Romans 5:8-9).

To the believer is given this responsibility relating to being a light to the world. This then is a call to seeking purity as God is pure, to living according to the moral, ethical and spiritual values of God's Word, and to demonstrating the sacrificial love of Christ.

Even as thunder is impressive but lightning does the work, so talk from Christians can be impressive; nevertheless, it's the light that penetrates. That light is Jesus, living through a surrendered life, shining on a darkened world. The beauty of the principle is that while the light of Christ shines through a life, that life is also blessed. As Sir James Barrie said, "Those who bring sunshine to the lives of others cannot keep it from themselves."

Christian friend, you may be the only light from God that some people see, so don't hide your light under a bushel (Matthew 5:15). Let the world around you see the purity of God, the values of scripture and the love of Christ. Don't just make noise, be a light.

Personal Notes:

December 9
Jeremiah 3:20-4:2

Surely, as a wife treacherously departs from her husband, so have you dealt treacherously with Me, O house of Israel," says the LORD. A voice was heard on the desolate heights, Weeping and supplications of the children of Israel. For they have perverted their way; They have forgotten the LORD their God. "Return, you backsliding children, And I will heal your backslidings." "Indeed we do come to You, For You are the LORD our God. Truly, in vain is salvation hoped for from the hills, And from the multitude of mountains; Truly, in the LORD our God Is the salvation of Israel. For shame has devoured the labour of our fathers from our youth—Their flocks and their herds, their sons and their daughters. We lie down in our shame, and our reproach covers us. For we have sinned against the LORD our God, We and our fathers, From our youth even to this day, and have not obeyed the voice of the LORD our God."

"If you will return, O Israel," says the LORD, "Return to Me; And if you will put away your abominations out of My sight, Then you shall not be moved. And you shall swear, 'The LORD lives, in truth, in judgment, and in righteousness; The nations shall bless themselves in Him, And in Him they shall glory.'"

The Arena of Entertainment

In his book "Loving God", Charles Colson retells this story: "The Asian hermit lived in a remote village tending his garden and spending much time in prayer. One day he thought he heard the voice of God telling him to go to Rome, so he obeyed. Weary weeks later, he arrived in the city at the time of a great festival. The little monk followed the crowd surging down the streets into the Coliseum. He saw the gladiators stand before the emperor and say, "We who are about to die salute you." When he realized these men were going to fight to the death for the entertainment of the crowd. He cried out, "In the name of Christ, stop!"

As the games began he pushed his way through the crowd, and climbed over the wall. When the crowd saw this tiny figure rushing to the gladiators and repeating, "In the name of Christ, stop!" they thought it was part of the act and began laughing.

Soon laughter turned to anger. As he was pleading with the gladiators to stop, one of them plunged a sword into his body. He fell to the sand. As he was dying, his last words were, "In the name of Christ, stop!"

Then a strange thing happened. The gladiators stood looking at the tiny figure lying there. A hush fell over the Coliseum. Way up in the upper rows, a man stood and made his way to the exit. Others began to follow. In dead silence, everyone left the Coliseum.

The year was A.D. 391, and that was the last battle to the death between gladiators. Never again in the great stadium did men kill each other for the entertainment of the crowd, all because of one tiny voice. One voice, one life, that spoke the truth in God's name."

Although there may be no such thing as "gladiator games" in today's arena of entertainment, there is still much death. There is the death of the family at the hands of an entertainment philosophy which portrays immorality and violence as the happy norm. There is the death of honesty and integrity by a sport's philosophy which pushes "win at all cost". There is the death of childhood at the hands of parental madness which cries: "Performance!", "Accomplishment!", "Achieve! Achieve!"

Into this entertainment frenzy, a small voice is wanting, a tiny figure needed to cry "In the name of Christ, stop!" Jeremiah's message bears repeating: "If you will return, O Israel, return to me," declares the LORD. "If you put your detestable idols out of my sight and no longer go astray, and if in a truthful, just and righteous way you swear, `As surely as the LORD lives,' then the nations will be blessed by him and in him they will glory."(Jeremiah 4:1-2 NIV)

There is a need in every community for the bells to again ring, calling people to come and worship the Prince of Peace, to turn back to God.

Personal Notes:

December 10
Luke 15:1-10

Then all the tax collectors and the sinners drew near to Him to hear Him. And the Pharisees and scribes complained, saying, "This Man receives sinners and eats with them." So He spoke this parable to them, saying: "What man of you, having a hundred sheep, if he loses one of them, does not leave the ninety-nine in the wilderness, and go after the one which is lost until he finds it? "And when he has found it, he lays it on his shoulders, rejoicing. "And when he comes home, he calls together his friends and neighbours, saying to them, 'Rejoice with me, for I have found my sheep which was lost!' "I say to you that likewise there will be more joy in heaven over one sinner who repents than over ninety-nine just persons who need no repentance. "Or what woman, having ten silver coins, if she loses one coin, does not light a lamp, sweep the house, and search carefully until she finds it? "And when she has found it, she calls her friends and neighbours together, saying, 'Rejoice with me, for I have found the piece which I lost!' "Likewise, I say to you, there is joy in the presence of the angels of God over one sinner who repents."

Burst of Joy

When the Pulitzer Prizes for national reporting were awarded in 1974, the feature photography award went to Sal Veder of the Associated Press for his photo of former prisoner of war, Lt.-Col. Robert Stirm, being greeted by his family on his return to the United States. Veder entitled his photo "Burst of Joy". The absence of the head of that family was keenly felt during his imprisonment. His return was reason for celebration.

How sad it is that the same could not be said for the return of the living God among His creation. When sin separated man from intimate fellowship with God, Adam and Eve sensed the great loss. However, each successive generation of man seems to have felt that loss less. Now, complete denial of the existence of God has become socially acceptable.

Although God has dealt specifically with individuals throughout history, not until God became man was such intimacy between God and man made available again. The great miracle of the conception of the Christ child is recorded in scriptures. To the

144

virgin, Mary, God sent this message: "The Holy Ghost shall come upon you, and the power of the Highest shall overshadow you: therefore, also that holy thing which shall be born of you shall be called the Son of God." (Luke 1:35)

Mary appreciated the wonder of the miracle and her own great privilege: "And Mary said: "My soul glorifies the Lord and my spirit rejoices in God my Saviour" (Luke 1:46-47 NIV). When the child was born, the angels announced the event with celebration: "Suddenly a great company of the heavenly host appeared with the angel, praising God and saying, "Glory to God in the highest, and on earth peace to men on whom his favour rests." (Luke 2:13-14 NIV) The shepherds who received the announcement responded with celebration: "The shepherds returned, glorifying and praising God for all the things they had heard and seen" (Luke 2:20 NIV) The wise men travelled many miles to celebrate the event in worship: "When they saw the star, they were overjoyed. On coming to the house, they saw the child with his mother Mary, and they bowed down and worshipped him." (Matthew 2 NIV). Dedicated Simeon rejoiced and Anna the prophetess celebrated with joy (Luke 2).

Nevertheless, the great horde of mankind took little notice of God's coming. As a matter of fact the Bible indicates that there was a general feeling of apathy and rejection, even among those who were confronted with proof of His Deity: "The true light that gives light to every man was coming into the world. He was in the world...He came to that which was his own, but his own did not receive him." (John 1 NIV)

Christ returned to provide freedom for man. His birth is reason to celebrate in joy and worship. What better way is there to celebrate than to turn to Him for life? (see John 3:16) For each person who does, there is in heaven an angelic "Burst of Joy."

Personal Notes:

December 11
Jeremiah 17:1-10

"The sin of Judah is written with a pen of iron; with the point of a diamond it is engraved on the tablet of their heart, and on the horns of your altars, while their children remember their altars and their wooden images By the green trees on the high hills. O My mountain in the field, I will give as plunder your wealth, all your treasures, and your high places of sin within all your borders. And you, even yourself, Shall let go of your heritage which I gave you; and I will cause you to serve your enemies In the land which you do not know; For you have kindled a fire in My anger which shall burn forever." Thus says the LORD: "Cursed is the man who trusts in man and makes flesh his strength, whose heart departs from the LORD. For he shall be like a shrub in the desert, and shall not see when good comes, but shall inhabit the parched places in the wilderness, in a salt land which is not inhabited. "Blessed is the man who trusts in the LORD, and whose hope is the LORD. For he shall be like a tree planted by the waters, which spreads out its roots by the river, and will not fear when heat comes; But its leaf will be green, and will not be anxious in the year of drought, nor will cease from yielding fruit. "The heart is deceitful above all things, And desperately wicked; Who can know it? I, the LORD, search the heart, I test the mind, Even to give every man according to his ways, According to the fruit of his doings.

Heart Condition

In all this beauty of snow covered towns and forest, blanketed in sparkling wonder, it's hard to imagine that tragedy awaits. I refer to the inevitable heart attack victims who overexert themselves in an effort to clear driveways, or push cars out of snow drifts. Often without realizing they have weakened hearts, these unsuspecting people are caught unaware. Then tragedy strikes, changing their lives permanently. From that moment on, the world labels these folks as "having a heart condition".

The tragic connotation of this phrase is true of every person, in a spiritual sense. The Old Testament book of Jeremiah has a lot to say about the heart. Mentioned some 58 times, the heart is described as evil, wicked, scheming, calloused, deceitful, covetous, proud, lying, and turned away from God.

Only God can change this heart condition. For this very reason He sent His Son to earth as the Saviour of the world. For all who will put their trust in Him, confessing their sin and accepting Christ's death on the cross as substitution for the divine penalty of personal sin, God renews the heart with His own life. The "heart blessings" of salvation which will be true of a whole nation, are true of the individual believer as well: "I will give you a new heart and put a new spirit in you". (Ezekiel 36:26 NIV)

Of this changed heart condition Charles Spurgeon wrote: "The hard heart does not love the Redeemer, but the renewed heart burns with affection towards him. Many are the privileges of this renewed heart: "Tis here the Spirit dwells, tis here that Jesus rests." It is fitted to receive every heavenly fruit to the honour and praise of God, and therefore the Lord delights in it. A tender heart is the best defence against sin, and the best preparation for heaven. A renewed heart stands on its water tower looking for the coming of the Lord Jesus."

In the midst of all the beauty of winter's wonderland declaring the handiwork of God (Psalm 19:1) and reminding us of all His gifts (James 1:17), there is still the tragedy of the condition of the human heart. God has an answer for that condition: "And this is the testimony: God has given us eternal life, and this life is in his Son. He who has the Son has life; he who does not have the Son of God does not have life." (1 John 5:11-12 NIV)

With this new life, there comes a renewed heart. What is your "spiritual" heart condition; turned from God or renewed in God?

Personal Notes:

December 12

Psalm 51:1-13

Have mercy upon me, O God, According to Your lovingkindness; According to the multitude of Your tender mercies, Blot out my transgressions. Wash me thoroughly from my iniquity, and cleanse me from my sin. For I acknowledge my transgressions and my sin is always before me. Against You, You only, have I sinned, and done this evil in Your sight—That You may be found just when You speak, And blameless when You judge. Behold, I was brought forth in iniquity, and in sin my mother conceived me. Behold, You desire truth in the inward parts, And in the hidden part You will make me to know wisdom.

Purge me with hyssop, and I shall be clean; Wash me, and I shall be whiter than snow. Make me hear joy and gladness, that the bones You have broken may rejoice. Hide Your face from my sins, And blot out all my iniquities. Create in me a clean heart, O God, and renew a steadfast spirit within me. Do not cast me away from Your presence, and do not take Your Holy Spirit from me. Restore to me the joy of Your salvation, and uphold me by Your generous Spirit. Then I will teach transgressors Your ways, And sinners shall be converted to You.

A Deadly Bug Bite

According to Annie Dillard, in her book, "Pilgrim at Tinker Creek", a giant water bug can with a single bite paralyse its victims, be they insects, tadpoles, frogs or fish. By injecting a poison that dissolves into liquid muscles, bones and organs, this beetle can literally drain the life out of its victims.

Lust, which is God-given desire, directed outside of God's defined parameters, is a similar poison to the soul. James states: "...each one is tempted when, by his own evil desire, he is dragged away and enticed. Then, after desire has conceived, it gives birth to sin; and sin, when it is full-grown, gives birth to death." (James 1 NIV).

James is making a general statement regarding the source of temptation and its consequence when succumbed to. In his book, "Be Mature", Warren Wiersbe offers a clear explanation of this text: "The normal desires of life were given to us by God and, of themselves, are not sinful. Without these desires, we could not function. Unless we felt hunger and thirst, we would never eat and drink, and we would die. Without fatigue, the body would never rest. It is when we want to satisfy these desires in ways outside God's will that we get into trouble. Eating is normal; gluttony is sin. Sleep is normal; laziness is sin. "Marriage is honourable in all, and the bed undefiled: but whoremongers and adulterers God will judge." Hebrews 13:4.

  The beauty of God's goodness is that He has made provision for each person to be forgiven: "But God commendeth his love toward us, in that, while we were yet sinners, Christ died for us. Much more then, being now justified by his blood, we shall be saved from wrath through him... if thou shalt confess with thy mouth the Lord Jesus, and shalt believe in thine heart that God hath raised him from the dead, thou shalt be saved. For with the heart man believeth unto righteousness; and with the mouth confession is made unto salvation." (Romans 5:8-9, Romans 10:9-10).

  As well, for those who turn to God in faith, He guarantees strength and escape for temptation: "There hath no temptation taken you but such as is common to man: but God is faithful, who will not suffer you to be tempted above that ye are able; but will with the temptation also make a way to escape, that ye may be able to bear it." (1 Corinthians 10:13).

  The sin bug has bitten every person, the poison that destroys is in the heart of man from birth, but the grace of God provides new life in Christ. Have you taken God's antidote for sin?

Personal Notes:

December 13

Psalm 28:1-9

To You I will cry, O LORD my Rock: Do not be silent to me, Lest, if You are silent to me, I become like those who go down to the pit. Hear the voice of my supplications when I cry to You, When I lift up my hands toward Your holy sanctuary. Do not take me away with the wicked And with the workers of iniquity, Who speak peace to their neighbours, But evil is in their hearts. Give them according to their deeds, And according to the wickedness of their endeavours; Give them according to the work of their hands; Render to them what they deserve. Because they do not regard the works of the LORD, nor the operation of His hands, He shall destroy them And not build them up.

Blessed be the LORD, Because He has heard the voice of my supplications!

The LORD is my strength and my shield; My heart trusted in Him, and I am helped; Therefore my heart greatly rejoices, And with my song I will praise Him. The LORD is their strength, And He is the saving refuge of His anointed. Save Your people, And bless Your inheritance; Shepherd them also, And bear them up forever.

Pulling Strength

Here is an amusing story: "A man ran his car into the ditch. Fortunately, a passing farmer came along and offered help with his work horse. He hitched the horse to the car and yelled, "Pull, Nellie, pull!" The horse didn't move. Then the farmer hollered, "Pull, Clyde, pull!" No response! Once more the farmer commanded "Pull, Sam, pull!" Nothing. Then the farmer nonchalantly said, "Pull, Bess, pull!" And the horse easily dragged the car out of the ditch.

The motorist was most appreciative and very curious, so he asked the farmer which was the horse's real name. The farmer said, "Oh, Bess is her real name, but the horse is blind you know! And if Bess thought she was the only one pulling, she wouldn't even try!"

Life is filled with challenges that require the discipline of a good strong effort. Often such challenges as a death in the family, a severed relationship, a lost job or business failure, present themselves as so formidable that any effort to overcome would seem hopeless. Christians are not exempt from such challenges, nor from the reality of such feelings. Yet, how like that horse, some Christians are blind to the ever present help of God, and "refuse to pull" themselves up and get on with life!

Paul faced challenges that few believers ever will, he faced the stress of physical circumstances (see 2 Corinthians 11:23-27, 12:7-8), of personal cares (see 2 Corinthians 2:12-13, 11:28), of pressing confrontation (see 2 Corinthians 6:8, 10:10, 11:5) and ultimately prison confinement (see Ephesians 3:1, 4:1, 6:20). In these passages Paul speaks of ship wrecks, beatings, wrongful accusations, missing associates, and troubling sickness. Yet Paul continued to pick himself up and press on: "this one thing I do, forgetting those things which are behind, and reaching forth unto those things which are before, I press toward the mark for the prize of the high calling of God in Christ Jesus. (Philippians 3:13-14).

And how could Paul continue under such circumstances? Paul never lost sight of the One who "pulled with Him". This was no imaginary help, no trick to the blind, this was God himself who said: "I will never leave you nor forsake you" (Joshua 1:5). Paul rejoiced to share the wonderful truth that was his own experience: "I can do all things through Christ which strengthens me." (Philippians 4:13)

Christian friend, are you facing the challenges of life with a blind eye to God's help? Or can you rejoice with Paul who could pray: "Now unto him that is able to do exceeding abundantly above all that we ask or think, according to the power that works in us, unto him [be] glory... Amen" (Ephesians 3:20-21).

Personal Notes:

December 14
Isaiah 42:: 1-13

"Behold! My Servant whom I uphold, My Elect One in whom My soul delights! I have put My Spirit upon Him; He will bring forth justice to the Gentiles. He will not cry out, nor raise His voice, nor cause His voice to be heard in the street. A bruised reed He will not break, and smoking flax He will not quench; He will bring forth justice for truth. He will not fail nor be discouraged, Till He has established justice in the earth; and the coastlands shall wait for His law."

Thus says God the LORD, Who created the heavens and stretched them out, Who spread forth the earth and that which comes from it, Who gives breath to the people on it, And spirit to those who walk on it: "I, the LORD, have called You in righteousness, And will hold Your hand; I will keep You and give You as a covenant to the people, As a light to the Gentiles, To open blind eyes, To bring out prisoners from the prison, Those who sit in darkness from the prison house. I am the LORD, that is My name; And My glory I will not give to another, Nor My praise to carved images.

Behold, the former things have come to pass, and new things I declare; Before they spring forth I tell you of them." 0 Sing to the LORD a new song, And His praise from the ends of the earth, You who go down to the sea, and all that is in it, You coastlands and you inhabitants of them! Let the wilderness and its cities lift up their voice, The villages that Kedar inhabits. Let the inhabitants of Sela sing, Let them shout from the top of the mountains. Let them give glory to the LORD, and declare His praise in the coastlands.

The LORD shall go forth like a mighty man; He shall stir up His zeal like a man of war. He shall cry out, yes, shout aloud; He shall prevail against His enemies.

Two Advents

I recall the time when our family was amused by a photograph from our holidays. The photo was a beach scene of a family member holding a foot high person in his hand. It was only an optical illusion made possible by the trick of a camera which captured the close up of our family member with another person much farther down the beach, yet it appeared as though we were the first to photograph a person talking to a leprechaun!

That photo serves as a reminder of a similar mistaken view of Christ's advent. As Christ ministered almost 2000 years ago, he confronted the people's expectation of His coming to establish a World

Kingdom. During the triumphal entrance of Jesus into Jerusalem the people shouted: "Hosanna to the Son of David" (Matthew 21:9). This was a clear acknowledgement of Jesus as the Coming King and the very reason for the chief priests and scribes to become incensed.

Even after the Lord's resurrection the disciples asked about the expected reign: "When they therefore were come together, they asked of him, saying, Lord, wilt thou at this time restore again the kingdom to Israel?" (Acts 1:6).

These people knew the Old Testament promises of Christ's coming kingdom but failed to see Christ's coming suffering. They viewed two distinct events, separated by a period of time that only God knows, as one. Yet Christ's First advent was one of humility. He was conceived in a virgin, born in a barn, lived among the poor, ministered among the needy, and died for the world as a common criminal (see Isaiah 53).

The disciples could not at first reconcile this suffering Messiah with the prophecies of His glorious Kingdom of world peace where: "The wolf also shall dwell with the lamb, and the leopard shall lie down with the kid..."(Isaiah 11:6). However, through New Testament revelation, God clearly distinguished the Two Advents and prophesied that Jesus, who came with humiliation to suffer, will come again with vindication to rule: "And I saw heaven opened, and behold a white horse; and he that sat upon him was called Faithful and True, and in righteousness he doth judge and make war... And out of his mouth goeth a sharp sword, that with it he should smite the nations: and he shall rule them with a rod of iron: and he treadeth the winepress of the fierceness and wrath of Almighty God. And he hath on [his] vesture and on his thigh a name written, KING OF KINGS, AND LORD OF LORDS." (Revelation 19:11ff)

During this Advent period, remember that as sure as Jesus came before as a babe in a manger, He is coming again - to judge and to reign. Those who receive Him as Suffering Saviour, may soon see their King. Those who reject Him as Saviour will meet Him as judge! I urge each reader to appropriate His First Advent by repentance and faith, that you may anticipate with joy and peace, His Second Coming.

Personal Notes:

December 15
Romans 8:32-39

What then shall we say to these things? If God is for us, who can be against us? He who did not spare His own Son, but delivered Him up for us all, how shall He not with Him also freely give us all things? Who shall bring a charge against God's elect? It is God who justifies. Who is he who condemns? It is Christ who died, and furthermore is also risen, who is even at the right hand of God, who also makes intercession for us. Who shall separate us from the love of Christ? Shall tribulation, or distress, or persecution, or famine, or nakedness, or peril, or sword? As it is written: "For Your sake we are killed all day long; We are accounted as sheep for the slaughter." Yet in all these things we are more than conquerors through Him who loved us. For I am persuaded that neither death nor life, nor angels nor principalities nor powers, nor things present nor things to come, nor height nor depth, nor any other created thing, shall be able to separate us from the love of God which is in Christ Jesus our Lord.

Quest for Love

There is a quest today among mankind that is more significant than Columbus's search for a new world, more costly than science's pursuit of space. It is a quest that has made superficial heroes out of movie stars, cultic idols out of singers, millionaires out of romance novelists. It is a quest that has rightfully called young people to leave their homes in pursuit of life partners; it is a quest that has wrongfully perverted God ordained human intimacy. It is a quest that has turned both the legal profession and the pet industry to multibillion dollar profits. It is a quest for love.

The world cries out "I want to be loved!" And though it knows little of the real meaning of love, it nonetheless thirsts after it as a rushing deer seeks the fresh water of a forest brook. How sad it is that the very source that quenches this thirst is so much ignored.

The apostle John reminds us that "God is love" (1 John 4:16). He also reminds us of the greatest expression of God's love: "This is how God showed his love among us: He sent his one and only Son into the world that we might live through him" (1 John 4:9 NIV). It was out of love for mankind that God sent forth His Son to be conceived in a virgin and born as a man. It was out of love that the child was born in poverty and lived in humility. It was out of love that God gave His Son as a sacrifice for the sin of the world, and it is out of love that God grants forgiveness and eternal life to all who confess and believe: "For God so loved the world, that he gave his only begotten Son, that whosoever believeth in him should not perish, but have everlasting life" (John 3:16).

During the Christmas season this failed quest for love is felt the keenest in people's hearts, and often the resultant hurt and unquenched thirst is pushed aside with the business celebration. Yet God would have mankind remember that the centre of the celebrations - the Christ Child, is the very point of the quest for love's end!

For the unconditional love of man, the child in the cradle became the Son on the cross. It was He who said: "If anyone is thirsty, let him come to me and drink. Whoever believes in me, as the Scripture has said, streams of living water will flow from within him" (John 7 NIV).

In our mind's eye, let this prayer be written across the manger scene: "I bow my knees to the Father... that Christ may dwell in your hearts by faith; that you, being rooted and grounded in love, may be able to comprehend with all saints what is the breadth, and length, and depth, and height; And to know the love of Christ, which passes knowledge, that you might be filled with all the fullness of God" (Ephesians 3).

Personal Notes:

December 16
2 Corinthians 4:1-10

Therefore, since we have this ministry, as we have received mercy, we do not lose heart. But we have renounced the hidden things of shame, not walking in craftiness nor handling the word of God deceitfully, but by manifestation of the truth commending ourselves to every man's conscience in the sight of God. But even if our gospel is veiled, it is veiled to those who are perishing, whose minds the god of this age has blinded, who do not believe, lest the light of the gospel of the glory of Christ, who is the image of God, should shine on them. For we do not preach ourselves, but Christ Jesus the Lord, and ourselves your bondservants for Jesus' sake. For it is the God who commanded light to shine out of darkness, who has shone in our hearts to give the light of the knowledge of the glory of God in the face of Jesus Christ. But we have this treasure in earthen vessels that the excellence of the power may be of God and not of us.

We are hard pressed on every side, yet not crushed; we are perplexed, but not in despair; persecuted, but not forsaken; struck down, but not destroyed— always carrying about in the body the dying of the Lord Jesus, that the life of Jesus also may be manifested in our body.

Suffering with Expectation

Philip Yancey concludes his book "Where is God When it Hurts?" with this thought: "In one sense, there will be no solution to pain unit Jesus returns and recreates the earth. I am sustained by faith in that great hope. If I did not truly believe that God is a Physician and not a Sadist, and that He "feels in Himself the tortured presence of every nerve that lacks its repose," I would immediately abandon all attempts to plumb the mysteries of suffering."

Hope presses the believer to expect more from God! This was evident in Paul's life as he expressed his own attitude toward suffering in the Second Epistle of Corinthians. Paul makes reference to three specific expectations of suffering. First and foremost, he expects to see God glorified: "For we which live are always delivered unto death for Jesus' sake, that the life also of Jesus might be made manifest in our mortal flesh. So then death works in us, but life in you... For all things are for your sakes, that the abundant grace might through the thanksgiving of many redound to the glory of God" (2 Corinthians 12:11-15).

The heart beat of Paul was to see God glorified as the One True God, all-sufficient in times of trial and distress. Paul had already alluded to this: "Not that we are sufficient of ourselves to think any thing as of ourselves; but our sufficiency is of God" (2 Corinthians 3:5).

Paul expresses a second expectation of suffering: "But we all, with open face beholding as in a glass the glory of the Lord, are changed into the same image from glory to glory, even as by the Spirit of the Lord" (2 Corinthians 3:18). Here Paul speaks of the practical affect of living by faith in the all sufficient God. The path of suffering that evidences human weakness, necessitates a deep dependency upon the provision of God. This deep dependency demands a close communion with God, which in turn, results in the transforming of a life into godlikeness. Paul speaks of practical sanctification, raised to a higher level by the sufferings of ministry: "For our light affliction, which is but for a moment, works for us a far more exceeding and eternal weight of glory" (2 Corinthians 4:17).

He expected to experience greater power: "And he said unto me, My grace is sufficient for thee: for my strength is made perfect in weakness. Most gladly therefore will I rather glory in my infirmities, that the power of Christ may rest upon me." (2 Corinthians 12:9-11). Paul, through sickness, weakness and suffering, was made more like Christ. Therefore, by grace, he was assured of more of the unique power of Christ in his life.

In suffering, the Christian finds hope in God being glorified, life being sanctified, strength being fortified; all this and heaven too! No wonder Paul could say "For me to live is Christ, and to die is gain!" (Philip. 1:21). Has your heart found such expectation in suffering?

Personal Notes:

December 17
Psalm 119:73-80

Your hands have made me and fashioned me; Give me understanding, that I may learn Your commandments. Those who fear You will be glad when they see me, Because I have hoped in Your word. I know, O LORD, that Your judgments are right, And that in faithfulness You have afflicted me. Let, I pray, Your merciful kindness be for my comfort, According to Your word to Your servant. Let Your tender mercies come to me, that I may live; For Your law is my delight. Let the proud be ashamed, For they treated me wrongfully with falsehood; But I will meditate on Your precepts. Let those who fear You turn to me, Those who know Your testimonies. Let my heart be blameless regarding Your statutes, That I may not be ashamed.

Suffering with Profit

In a famous study by Victor and Mildred Goertzel, entitled "Cradles of Eminence", the home backgrounds of 300 highly successful people were investigated. These 300 subjects had made it to the top. They were men and women whose names everyone would recognize as brilliant in their fields; names such as Franklin D. Roosevelt, Helen Keller, Winston Churchill, Albert Schweitzer, Clara Barton, Gandhi, Einstein, and Freud. The intensive investigation into their early home lives yielded some surprising findings.

Three fourths of the children were troubled either by poverty, by a broken home, or by rejecting, over-possessive, or dominating parents. Seventy-four of 85 writers of fiction or drama and 16 of the 20 poets came from homes where, as children, they saw tense psychological drama played out by their parents. Physical handicaps such as blindness, deafness, or crippled limbs characterized over one-fourth of the sample. How did these people go on, then, to such outstanding accomplishments? Most likely it was by compensation. They compensated for their weaknesses in one area by excelling in another.

The famous blind songwriter Fanny Crosby wrote more than 8,000 songs. This fact and other interesting highlights in the life of Miss Crosby were revealed by Warren Wiersbe in his book "Victorious Christian." Wiersbe explained that when Fanny was only 6 weeks old a minor eye inflammation developed. The doctor who treated the case was careless though, and she became totally and permanently blind. Fanny Crosby harboured no bitterness against the physician, however. In fact, she once said of him, "If I could meet him now, I would say thank you, over and over again for making me blind." She felt that her blindness was a gift from God to help her write the hymns that flowed from her pen. According to those who knew her, Miss Crosby probably would have refused treatment even if it could have assured the restoration of her sight.

Wiersbe concluded by commenting: "It was said of another blind hymn-writer, George Matheson, that God made him blind so he could see clearly in other ways and become a guide to men. This same tribute could be applied to Fanny Crosby, who triumphed over her handicap and used it to the glory of God." Yes, this talented woman allowed her tragedy to make her better instead of bitter.

Early in life David, the Psalmist learned: "I know, O LORD, that thy judgments are right, and that thou in faithfulness hast afflicted me" (Psalms 119:75). Have you reader learned the same? Can you say: "I rejoice in knowing that... There is no oil without squeezing the olives, no wine without pressing the grapes, no fragrance without crushing the flowers, and no real joy without sorrow."

Personal Notes:

December 18
Luke 8:9-15

When His disciples asked Him, saying, "What does this parable mean?" And He said, "To you it has been given to know the mysteries of the kingdom of God, but to the rest it is given in parables, that 'Seeing they may not see, and hearing they may not understand.' "Now the parable is this: The seed is the word of God. "Those by the wayside are the ones who hear; then the devil comes and takes away the word out of their hearts, lest they should believe and be saved. "But the ones on the rock are those who, when they hear, receive the word with joy; and these have no root, who believe for a while and in time of temptation fall away. "Now the ones that fell among thorns are those who, when they have heard, go out and are choked with cares, riches, and pleasures of life, and bring no fruit to maturity. "But the ones that fell on the good ground are those who, having heard the word with a noble and good heart, keep it and bear fruit with patience.

Persevering in Purity

In December of 1998 the hearts of Canadians reached out in sympathy with the drowning death of Michel Trudeau, son of Prime Minister Trudeau. That this young adventurer was last seen struggling with the weight of his ski equipment in the icy waters impresses our minds with scenes of panic, as we join with those onlookers in helpless horror. Young Trudeau met his death in a manner common to many in our area where thin ice conditions and heavy clothing conspire to make an end of life.

Christians are called upon to guard against a spiritually parallel tragedy where the weight of sin can stifle the life of Christ within the believer. Christians are urged: "Wherefore seeing we also are compassed about with so great a cloud of witnesses, let us lay aside every weight, and the sin which doth so easily beset us, and let us run with patience the race that is set before us, Looking unto Jesus the author and finisher of our faith; who for the joy that was set before him endured the cross, despising the shame, and is set down at the right hand of the throne of God" (Hebrews 12:1-2).

Believers are here reminded first, of the inspiration to be guarded. There are a host of saints in glory (referred to in Hebrews 11) who are witnesses to the blessings of perseverance. Second, of the instruction for being guarded; they are to run with endurance a straight, clean race. Paul states the same in these words: "Do you not know that in a race all the runners run, but only one gets the prize? Run in such a way as to get the prize" (1 Corinthians 9:24 NIV). Thirdly, the believer is reminded of the image of guarding: they are to look to Jesus. Jesus persevered unto death, and as the giver of life through faith in him, he equips the Christian with the same power of perseverance he himself possesses. Lastly, the believer is reminded of the incentive for guarding- the joy of labour completed, which brings eternal reward (see 2 Timothy 4:7-8).

Nevertheless, many believers allow themselves to be bogged down with sin as they follow the moral slide of society. Robert Bork captures this path with the title of his book "Slouching Towards Gomorrah." Christians are accepting as norm, the moral corruptness of society, forgetting that God's Holiness is changeless, and what He deems sin, regardless of man's sliding standard, is still sin.

Dear Christian friend, God calls you to set aside sin and raise the standard high: "...Do not be deceived: Neither the sexually immoral nor idolaters nor adulterers nor male prostitutes nor homosexual offenders nor thieves nor the greedy nor drunkards nor slanderers nor swindlers will inherit the kingdom of God. And that is what some of you were. But you were washed, you were sanctified, you were justified in the name of the Lord Jesus Christ and by the Spirit of our God" (1 Corinthians 6:9-11 NIV).

Don't let sin drown your effectiveness for Christ!

Personal Notes:

December 19

1 Peter 1:13-25

Therefore gird up the loins of your mind, be sober, and rest your hope fully upon the grace that is to be brought to you at the revelation of Jesus Christ; as obedient children, not conforming yourselves to the former lusts, as in your ignorance; but as He who called you is holy, you also be holy in all your conduct, because it is written, "Be holy, for I am holy." And if you call on the Father, who without partiality judges according to each one's work, conduct yourselves throughout the time of your stay here in fear; knowing that you were not redeemed with corruptible things, like silver or gold, from your aimless conduct received by tradition from your fathers, but with the precious blood of Christ, as of a lamb without blemish and without spot. He indeed was foreordained before the foundation of the world, but was manifest in these last times for you who through Him believe in God, who raised Him from the dead and gave Him glory, so that your faith and hope are in God. Since you have purified your souls in obeying the truth through the Spirit in sincere love of the brethren, love one another fervently with a pure heart, having been born again, not of corruptible seed but incorruptible, through the word of God which lives and abides forever, because "All flesh is as grass, And all the glory of man as the flower of the grass. The grass withers, And its flower falls away, but the word of the LORD endures forever." Now this is the word which by the gospel was preached to you.

What the World Needs Now

Columnist Mark Steyn captured the dark state of society's moral ethic in his National Post article entitled "Lights, Camera, Death" (Saturday, December 12, 1998). Here he cited the television coverage of an assisted suicide, the American Civil Liberties Union opposition to the respectful burial of aborted babies, and a teenager's calloused delivery and immediate garbage disposal of her newborn in the ladies washroom during a school dance. Is there any doubt to human degradation, to human spiritual lostness and bondage to sin?

With acknowledgement of a living and Holy God, true honest reflection will join with John Bunyan who said: "Sin and corruption would bubble up out of my heart as naturally as water bubbles up out of a fountain. I thought now that everyone had a better heart than I had. I could have changed hearts with anybody.

I thought none but the devil himself could equal me for inward wickedness and pollution of mind."

It was into this sin bound world that the Son of God came to bring deliverance. Zacharias prophesied of Christ's unique mission: "Blessed be the Lord God of Israel; for he hath visited and redeemed his people, And hath raised up an horn of salvation for us in the house of his servant David" (Luke 1:68-69). In Christ is seen God's passion for delivering mankind; "to visit" is to look upon in order to help. The Bible is filled with evidence of God's agony and timely intervention for man's in trouble. The greatest expression of this is the sending of His Son to die for man: "But God commendeth his love toward us, in that, while we were yet sinners, Christ died for us" (Romans 5:8).

Zacharias's words also reveal the price of mankind's deliverance; The Son would "redeem" his people. To redeem is literally to pay a ransom, that ransom was Christ's substitutional death for man: "For you know that it was not with perishable things such as silver or gold that you were redeemed… but with the precious blood of Christ, a lamb without blemish or defect" (1 Peter 1:18-19 NIV). Zacharias also expressed the power of Christ's deliverance as "a horn of salvation." The horn of rams or cattle was a cultural expression of power or might. Christ's power of deliverance was evidenced through His resurrection from the dead, by which he has secured a believer's full pardon and forgiveness (Romans 4:25).

The real message of Christmas peace begins with the understanding and acceptance of Jesus Christ's work of salvation. The cradle is meaningless without the cross! Man's deplorable fallen state must be dealt with before Holy God. To this end Jesus came, as John Bunyan also declared: "Far better news the Gospel brings. It bids us fly and gives us wings. Doubt not his sacrifice can save. God sealed it with an empty grave. And by his blood and life we live, and now have freedom to forgive."

And the angels said "Glory to God in the highest, and on earth peace, good will toward men" (Luke 2:14).

Personal Notes:

December 20
Isaiah 8:20-9:7

To the law and to the testimony! If they do not speak according to this word, it is because there is no light in them. They will pass through it hard pressed and hungry; and it shall happen, when they are hungry, that they will be enraged and curse their king and their God, and look upward. Then they will look to the earth, and see trouble and darkness, gloom of anguish; and they will be driven into darkness. Nevertheless the gloom will not be upon her who is distressed, As when at first He lightly esteemed The land of Zebulun and the land of Naphtali, And afterward more heavily oppressed her, By the way of the sea, beyond the Jordan, In Galilee of the Gentiles. The people who walked in darkness have seen a great light; Those who dwelt in the land of the shadow of death, Upon them a light has shined. You have multiplied the nation and increased its joy; They rejoice before You According to the joy of harvest, As men rejoice when they divide the spoil. For You have broken the yoke of his burden And the staff of his shoulder, The rod of his oppressor, As in the day of Midian. For every warrior's sandal from the noisy battle, And garments rolled in blood, Will be used for burning and fuel of fire. For unto us a Child is born, Unto us a Son is given; And the government will be upon His shoulder. And His name will be called Wonderful, Counsellor, Mighty God, Everlasting Father, Prince of Peace. Of the increase of His government and peace there will be no end, Upon the throne of David and over His kingdom, To order it and establish it with judgment and justice From that time forward, even forever. The zeal of the LORD of hosts will perform this.

Jesus – Out of Place!

Christmas time brings out the best of choral singing. Voices blend together in celebration of the birth of Christ as well as the joys of the season from the basses and baritones to the tenors and tweety-birds. Oops - it seems as though "tweety-bird" is rather out of place when referring to the harmony of choral singing. Yet, when you think about it, the entire Christmas story has an "out of place" theme.

Consider for a moment the prophecy of Isaiah about the Christ child's birth: "Therefore the Lord himself will give you a sign: The virgin will be with child and will give birth to a son, and will call him Immanuel" (Isaiah 7:14 NIV). Without doubt, this is an announcement of great scientific importance - a virgin having a child! You would have thought that even 2000 years ago the event would have drawn enough attention to guarantee accommodation wherever Mary went. How out of place it was for there to be no room at the inn!

Consider also Isaiah's prophecy about the Christ child himself: "For to us a child is born, to us a son is given, and the government will be on his shoulders. And he will be called Wonderful Counsellor, Mighty God, Everlasting Father, Prince of Peace." (Isaiah 9:6 NIV). Surely a child being born among men who is God himself deserved the very best of royal care and ceremony at His arrival. No monarchy ever born could possess such authority, and claim such royal heritage. You would think that some palace could have been made ready for the occasion. For such a child to be born in a barn seems very out of place!

Could it be that God was trying to send a message to mankind in these "out of place" circumstances? After all, The Son was sent because man had become out of place before God. Sin had separated all mankind from the place of life and fellowship with the Lord, ("for all have sinned and fall short of the glory of God," Romans 3:23 NIV).

God was declaring His own purpose of identifying with wayward man. The "out of place" birth of Christ only pointed to His coming "in man's place" death ("For Christ died for sins once for all, the righteous for the unrighteous, to bring you to God. He was put to death in the body but made alive by the Spirit," 1 Peter 3:18 NIV). God wanted mankind to realize that He is concerned with all people, even the very lowly people, the homeless, the helpless, those that are in physical and spiritual poverty.

If in the choral singing of Christmas you hear a squeaky, out of place voice (it probably will be my own), let it be a reminder of how God stepped "out of place" in order to put "back in place" those who believe on His name, ("Yet to all who received him, to those who believed in his name, he gave the right to become children of God" John 1:12 NIV).

Personal Notes:

December 21
Luke 2:1-7

And it came to pass in those days that a decree went out from Caesar Augustus that all the world should be registered. This census first took place while Quirinius was governing Syria. So all went to be registered, everyone to his own city. Joseph also went up from Galilee, out of the city of Nazareth, into Judea, to the city of David, which is called Bethlehem, because he was of the house and lineage of David, to be registered with Mary, his betrothed wife, who was with child. So it was, that while they were there, the days were completed for her to be delivered. And she brought forth her firstborn Son, and wrapped Him in swaddling cloths, and laid Him in a manger, because there was no room for them in the inn.

Christmas Island

In the Indian Ocean there is a Christmas Island, an almost lost, isolated speck of land. Christmas itself seems almost to be an isolated, lost island. From the first Christmas, which was celebrated in a barn because "there was no room in the inn," man has placed this miracle event in an out of way, quickly passed over place. Today's emphasis on commercialism has moved the truth of the event more remote than ever.

In "A Carol for Children" Ogden Nash picked up the rhythm of the carol "God Rest Ye Merry, Gentlemen" but began instead "God rest you, merry innocents." Two of the stanzas are these:

> "Oh, dimly, dimly glows the star
> Through the electric throng;
> The bidding in temple and bazaar
> Drowns out the silver song.
> Two ultimate laws alone we know,
> The ledger and the sword--
> So far away, so long ago
> We lost the infant Lord."

Ogden Nash has expressed in song what is evident in society: Christmas is an isolated, almost lost island.

Nevertheless, the wonder of the event still is a marvel to consider: "And the Word became flesh and dwelt among us, and we beheld His glory, the glory of the only begotten of the Father, full of grace and truth" (John 1:14). As Martin Luther explained, "We are not to ascend the study of the divine majesty before we have adequately understood this little infant. We are to ascend into heaven by that ladder which is placed before us, using those steps which God prepared and used. ... The Son of God does not want to be seen and found in heaven. Therefore he descended from heaven to this earth and came to us in our flesh. He placed himself in the womb of his mother, in her lap, and on the cross. And this is the ladder by which we are to ascend to God."

Although there were multitudes of the heavenly host to hymn the glory of God becoming man, there was only a motley group of shepherds to bow and worship, and a mother and her husband to look upon the face of God, lying in that manger. Yet by that event "the whole course of human history was changed. That is a truth as unassailable as any truth. Art, music, literature, Western culture itself with all its institutions and Western man's whole understanding of himself and his world--it is impossible to conceive how differently things would have turned out if that birth had not happened whenever, wherever, however it did. And there is a truth beyond that: for millions of people who have believed since, the birth of Jesus made possible not just a new way of understanding life but a new way of living it." (Frederick Buechner in *Listening to Your Life*).

Christmas is an island of hope in a world of despair, an island of love in a world of indifference, an island of giving in a self-centered world. Friend, come to Christmas Island!

Personal Notes:

December 22
Luke 2:8-14

Now there were in the same country shepherds living out in the fields, keeping watch over their flock by night. And behold, an angel of the Lord stood before them, and the glory of the Lord shone around them, and they were greatly afraid. Then the angel said to them, "Do not be afraid, for behold, I bring you good tidings of great joy which will be to all people. "For there is born to you this day in the city of David a Savior, who is Christ the Lord. "And this will be the sign to you: You will find a Babe wrapped in swaddling cloths, lying in a manger." And suddenly there was with the angel a multitude of the heavenly host praising God and saying: "Glory to God in the highest, And on earth peace, goodwill toward men!"

Echoes of the First Christmas

As with echoes which become distorted with distance and faint with time, so the announcement of Christ's birth has, for the most part, been lost to society. Scripture records that wonderful message brought to the shepherds by the Angels, "Behold I bring you good tidings of great joy which will be to all people for there is born to you this day, in a city of David a Saviour who is Christ the Lord." (Luke 2).

To a world in need God announced the birth of His Son as the Saviour for the world. Nature has taught mankind that death is the operating principle. Scripture records that death and destruction are the consequences of sin. The shepherds of Christ's day knew this all too well. They lived in a time of turmoil in which power-hungry people played games of death and destruction with the general public. This is confirmed in the census taken for tax purposes that brought Joseph and Mary to Bethlehem. This is evident in Herod's annihilation of all the male children two years of age and under, at the news of the birth of a king in Bethlehem.

To the shepherds, typical of the general public, who lived within a society completely vulnerable to the whims of its dictators, came good news of a Saviour, born to bring deliverance. This was reason for joy for all people, regardless of race or creed or social standing. It was in the birth of the Saviour - Christ Lord, that "Glory to God' was expressed by the Angels and peace and goodwill toward men, made possible among mankind.

Although the echo of that announcement has grown faint and distorted, the situation in society has not changed. Since mankind in Adam fell from grace, the consequences of death and destruction have ruled the world. September 11th 2001 has brought this closer to home in North America, than ever before. Our world needs to hear, with renewed clarity, the old message: "A Saviour is Born". He is a Saviour who when received by faith, can change the heart destined for death into a heart blossoming with peace and goodwill.

In the Indian Ocean there is a Christmas Island; an almost lost, isolated speck of land. There is another Christmas Island, an equally isolated speck of land almost lost in the Pacific Ocean. Christmas is always an island, an island of hope in a world of despair, an island of love in a world of indifference, an island of giving in a self-centred world, an island so capable of bringing an oasis of joy and peace in the midst of raging destruction, if only the message would be heard. As one poet has said, "Two ultimate laws alone we know, The ledger and the sword, So far away, so long ago - We lost the infant Lord."

Friend, will you hear the voice of the angels with clarity and ask the Saviour to enter your life, or will you let this echo of their message become distorted and faint as yet another season goes by?

Personal Notes:

December 23
Luke 2:8-20

Now there were in the same country shepherds living out in the fields, keeping watch over their flock by night. And behold, an angel of the Lord stood before them, and the glory of the Lord shone around them, and they were greatly afraid. Then the angel said to them, "Do not be afraid, for behold, I bring you good tidings of great joy which will be to all people. "For there is born to you this day in the city of David a Saviour, who is Christ the Lord. "And this will be the sign to you: You will find a Babe wrapped in swaddling cloth, lying in a manger." And suddenly there was with the angel a multitude of the heavenly host praising God and saying: "Glory to God in the highest, And on earth peace, goodwill toward men!" So it was, when the angels had gone away from them into heaven, the shepherds said to one another, "Let us now go to Bethlehem and see this thing that has come to pass, which the Lord has made known to us." And they came with haste and found Mary and Joseph, and the Babe lying in a manger. Now when they had seen Him, they made widely known the saying which was told them concerning this Child. And all those who heard it marvelled at those things which were told them by the shepherds. But Mary kept all these things and pondered them in her heart.
20 Then the shepherds returned, glorifying and praising God for all the things that they had heard and seen, as it was told them.

Colours of Christmas

Christmas is such a special, people-oriented time of year that most families try to capture those moments in film. Part of the Christmas tradition itself is viewing past Christmas celebrations. Although there were no cameras at that first Christmas scene, the scriptures paint clear scenes for us to reflect upon.

What becomes immediately obvious when our attention is focused upon these scenes is the marked contrast in how the Christ Child was received. In Luke the first scene is painted with the colour of indifference; "And she brought forth her firstborn son, and wrapped him in swaddling clothes, and laid him in a manger; because there was no room for them in the inn." (Luke 2:7). An opportunity to take best advantage of good business prompted the management of Bethlehem Inn to look with cool indifference at the circumstances of a needy couple. In marked contrast to this is the bright colour of jubilance in the scene of the shepherds; "And it came to pass, as the angels were gone away from them into heaven, the shepherds said one to another, Let us now go even unto Bethlehem, and see this thing which is come to pass, which the Lord hath made known unto us... And the shepherds returned, glorifying and praising God for all the things that they had heard and seen, as it was told unto them." (Luke 2:15,20).

In Matthew the scenes of the First Christmas are painted with equal contrast. Here the soft colour of reverence is evident as the wise men come from a far land to pay homage; "And when they were come into the house, they saw the young child with Mary his mother, and fell down, and worshipped him: and when they had opened their treasures, they presented unto him gifts; gold, and frankincense, and myrrh." (Matthew 2:11). This delicate hue of reverence is sharply contrasted by the dark scene at the palace where intolerance and hate fill the picture: "Then Herod, when he saw that he was mocked of the wise men, was exceeding wroth, and sent forth, and slew all the children that were in Bethlehem, and in all the coasts thereof, from two years old and under, according to the time which he had diligently enquired of the wise men." (Matthew 2:16).

As the scenes of that first Christmas are reflected upon, it becomes obvious that little has changed. The films and photos of our Christmas Celebrations are marked by the same contrasts of reception toward the Christ Child. If time is taken to consider the cause of the contrast, the answer comes readily. The contrast is caused by who is in the centre of the picture. Where man is in the centre, the scenes are filled with indifference and intolerance; where Christ is in the centre, jubilance and reverence are predominant. As much as Christmas time should be people-oriented, it must be Christ-centred. To focus otherwise is to miss the truth of Christmas: "For God sent not his Son into the world to condemn the world; but that the world through him might be saved." (John 3:17).

What colours fill the scenes of your Christmas, indifference and intolerance or jubilance and reverence?

Personal Notes:

December 24
Philippians 2:1-11

Therefore if there is any consolation in Christ, if any comfort of love, if any fellowship of the Spirit, if any affection and mercy, fulfil my joy by being like-minded, having the same love, being of one accord, of one mind. Let nothing be done through selfish ambition or conceit, but in lowliness of mind let each esteem others better than himself. Let each of you look out not only for his own interests, but also for the interests of others. Let this mind be in you which was also in Christ Jesus, who, being in the form of God, did not consider it robbery to be equal with God, but made Himself of no reputation, taking the form of a bondservant, and coming in the likeness of men. And being found in appearance as a man, He humbled Himself and became obedient to the point of death, even the death of the cross. Therefore, God also has highly exalted Him and given Him the name which is above every name, that at the name of Jesus every knee should bow, of those in heaven, and of those on earth, and of those under the earth, and that every tongue should confess that Jesus Christ is Lord, to the glory of God the Father.

What Child is This?

The question asked in the Christmas Carol "What Child is this?" is not only appropriate, but essential. While so much of our society embraces the holiday of Christmas, some even taking in the religious celebrations, often this question remains far from conscious consideration.

As Christmas morning dawns, before the hustle and bustle of wrapping paper and gift exchange, please take a moment and reflect upon The Child. The pages of scripture declare who He is: "Behold, a virgin shall be with child, and shall bring forth a son, and they shall call his name Emmanuel, which being interpreted is, God with us." (Matthew 1:23), "But when the fullness of the time was come, God sent forth his Son, made of a woman, made under the law," (Galatians 4:4).

Ponder the question; "What child is this, that so much of the world would celebrate His birth?", and consider the implications. If in our gaze upon the Child in the manger, our eyes fail to behold

"God Almighty" first and foremost, then our whole approach to Christmas is obstructed and our vision blurred!

To fail to see God Almighty, first and foremost, in that manger is to approach worship without God, is to sing praises without songs, is to toast a bride and groom without a marriage. To fail to see God Almighty in that manger is to leave open the doors of our lives to superficial religion, consuming materialism, personal indulgence, and meaningless activity that allow all manner of ungodliness to enter our hearts and hold us in bondage. To fail to see God Almighty in that manger is to fail to recognize the Saviour. "For unto you is born this day in the city of David a Saviour, which is Christ the Lord." (Luke 2:11). And to fail to recognize and personally believe in the Saviour is to fail to find God for Jesus said: "I am the way, the truth, and the life: no man cometh unto the Father, but by me." (John 14:6)

Read the words of the Christmas carol which has the answer as well as the question, and the essence of our proper response: "What Child is this, who, laid to rest, on Mary's lap is sleeping? Whom angels greet with anthems sweet, while shepherds watch are keeping? This, this is Christ the King, whom shepherds guard and angels sing: This, this is Christ the King, The Babe, the Son of Mary. So bring Him incense, gold and myrrh. Come, peasant, king, to own Him; The King of kings salvation brings, Let loving hearts enthrone Him."

Some think the Child was just a special prophet, others believe that through His achievements He became a god, but the old truth is still the only truth: "that Holy One who is to be born will be called the Son of God" (Luke 1:35), "And the Word was made flesh, and dwelt among us, (and we beheld his glory, the glory as of the only begotten of the Father,) full of grace and truth." (John 1:14).

Personal Notes:

December 25
Luke 2:1-14

And it came to pass in those days, that there went out a decree from Caesar Augustus, that all the world should be taxed. (And this taxing was first made when Cyrenius was governor of Syria.) And all went to be taxed, every one into his own city. And Joseph also went up from Galilee, out of the city of Nazareth, into Judaea, unto the city of David, which is called Bethlehem; (because he was of the house and lineage of David) To be taxed with Mary his espoused wife, being great with child. And so it was, that, while they were there, the days were accomplished that she should be delivered. And she brought forth her firstborn son, and wrapped him in swaddling clothes, and laid him in a manger; because there was no room for them in the inn.
And there were in the same country shepherds abiding in the field, keeping watch over their flock by night. And, lo, the angel of the Lord came upon them, and the glory of the Lord shone round about them: and they were sore afraid. And the angel said unto them, Fear not: for, behold, I bring you good tidings of great joy, which shall be to all people. For unto you is born this day in the city of David a Saviour, which is Christ the Lord. And this shall be a sign unto you; Ye shall find the babe wrapped in swaddling clothes, lying in a manger. And suddenly there was with the angel a multitude of the heavenly host praising God, and saying, Glory to God in the highest, and on earth peace, good will toward men.

Humble Birth of the Holy Child

It is reported that Abraham Lincoln visited one of his generals during the Civil War only to find him absent for a wedding. The general returned home late and went directly to bed without acknowledging the President at all. Lincoln's advisers urged the President to deliver the strongest reprimand; however Lincoln's response was very different: "I would hold McClellan's horse if he will only bring us success."

Such selflessness is most uncharacteristic of leaders today and quite against the flow of present day, self-centred, "I deserve better" thinking. With such selfishness prevalent, can man ever appreciate the selflessness of Christmas: "...Christ Jesus: Who, being in very nature God, did not consider equality with God something to be grasped, but made himself nothing,... being made in human likeness" (Philippians 2:5-7 NIV).

Should guarantee have been made that all the world would bow at Jesus' cradle, and all kingdoms would resign to his leadership, and all wealth would be brought to his doorstep, and all people would sit before Him in silent wonder, Jesus' birth would still have been the greatest act of selflessness of all time!

Consider what "becoming man" meant for the Son of God. It meant giving up heaven and becoming vulnerable to physical limitations such as hunger, fatigue, and even the common cold; it meant setting aside the recognizable glory of God at which all creatures must bow; it meant refusing his prerogative of power by burying His omnipotence in the will and purpose of the Father; it meant that the Lord of Glory restricted his presence and became confined to flesh and blood.

In just becoming man, Jesus forsook glory, honour, freedom, power, rights and privileges. Yet this text of Philippians continues the selfless humility of Christ from the cradle to the cross: "...taking the very nature of a servant, ... he humbled himself and became obedient to death--even death on a cross!" (Philippians 2:7-8 NIV).

In selflessness God became man, in continued selflessness as man, Jesus became a servant, (the word actually means slave). Jesus said: "For even the Son of Man did not come to be served, but to serve," (Mark 10:45 NIV). As a servant\slave Jesus became "the Lamb of God, who takes away the sin of the world!" (John 1:29 NIV).

Jesus came in selflessness, and calls all men by that same abandonment of self to receive Him, as Jesus said to Saul, "I have appeared to you to appoint you as a servant and as a witness of what you have seen of me ...I am sending you to them to open their eyes and turn them from darkness to light, and from the power of Satan to God, so that they may receive forgiveness of sins and a place among those who are sanctified by faith in me." (Acts 26:15-18 NIV).

Turning from darkness (repentance) to faith in Christ, is man's act of selfless abandonment. It is to say "I am unworthy, Jesus paid my debt". This Christmas, choose Christ!

Personal Notes:

December 26
Matthew 2:1-8

Now after Jesus was born in Bethlehem of Judea in the days of Herod the king, behold, wise men from the East came to Jerusalem, saying, "Where is He who has been born King of the Jews? For we have seen His star in the East and have come to worship Him." When Herod the king heard this, he was troubled, and all Jerusalem with him. And when he had gathered all the chief priests and scribes of the people together, he inquired of them where the Christ was to be born. So they said to him, "In Bethlehem of Judea, for thus it is written by the prophet: 'But you, Bethlehem, in the land of Judah, Are not the least among the rulers of Judah; For out of you shall come a Ruler Who will shepherd My people Israel.'" Then Herod, when he had secretly called the wise men, determined from them what time the star appeared. And he sent them to Bethlehem and said, "Go and search carefully for the young Child, and when you have found Him, bring back word to me, that I may come and worship Him also."

A Message in The Heavens.

The Christmas season is celebrated in various ways around the globe. One form of celebration that is growing in popularity is the "Festival of Lights". Not only is this an opportunity for man's creative instincts to shine with spectacular results, it is also fitting in its reminder of the star that announced the birth of the Christ child: "wise men from the east... asked, "Where is the one who has been born king of the Jews? We saw his star in the east and have come to worship him" (Matthew 2:2 NIV).

No matter how creatively spectacular man's celebrations become, they will all be dim before the Lord's. He marked Christ's birth with a special celestial light, a personal cosmic symbol, a burst of divine power and heavenly creativity to indicate the absolute uniqueness of the occasion. Although this was an ordinary birth, this was no ordinary child, for "when the time had fully come, God sent his Son, born of a woman" (Galatians 4:4 NIV). The child that was born that night in a lowly manger was God from before time began: "In the beginning was the Word, and the Word was with God, and the Word was God... The Word became flesh and made his dwelling among us. We have seen his glory, the glory of the One and Only, who came from the Father, full of grace and truth" (John 1:1,14 NIV).

C.S. Lewis, in his book *Mere Christianity*, states the wonder of this occasion: "The Second Person in God, The Son, became human himself: was born into the world as an actual man-a real man of particular height, with hair of a particular colour, speaking a particular language, weighing so many stone. The Eternal Being, who knows everything and who created the whole universe, became not only a man but a baby, and before that a fetus inside a Woman's body. If you want to get the hang of it, think how you would like to become a slug or a crab."

Paul expressed the dynamic of the occasion from the perspective of God: "Your attitude should be the same as that of Christ Jesus: Who, being in very nature God, did not consider equality with God something to be grasped" (Philippians 2:6 NIV). Paul, in giving an example of necessary Christian humility, marks the Son of God as the highest role model. He reminds the readers of the uniqueness of whom Jesus was in order to impress upon us the humility unsolved in what Jesus did: "but made himself nothing, taking the very nature of a servant, being made in human likeness" (Philippians 2:7 NIV).

God becoming man, the event was announced by a message in the heavens. It is sad that only the wise men from the east saw the star. Could it be that everyone else was too busy to take the time to look up? Isn't it true that today there are still very few "wise" people who recognize the message?

Personal Notes:

December 27

2 Peter 3:1-9

Beloved, I now write to you this second epistle (in both of which I stir up your pure minds by way of reminder),that you may be mindful of the words which were spoken before by the holy prophets, and of the commandment of us, the apostles of the Lord and Saviour, knowing this first: that scoffers will come in the last days, walking according to their own lusts, and saying, "Where is the promise of His coming? For since the fathers fell asleep, all things continue as they were from the beginning of creation." For this they wilfully forget: that by the word of God the heavens were of old, and the earth standing out of water and in the water, by which the world that then existed perished, being flooded with water. But the heavens and the earth which are now preserved by the same word, are reserved for fire until the day of judgment and perdition of ungodly men. But, beloved, do not forget this one thing, that with the Lord one day is as a thousand years, and a thousand years as one day. The Lord is not slack concerning His promise, as some count slackness, but is longsuffering toward us, not willing that any should perish but that all should come to repentance.

Willingness

And now we come to the "What I really wanted" season! This is that time when all thought of the care and love expressed toward us with that very special gift is often cast aside for an exchanged gift of higher priority. How the store clerks must smile within themselves at all the excuses they hear for returned items. The amazing thing to me is that stores are so willing to let items be returned or exchanged at all! In this perhaps the mood of Christmas is still alive, captured in that little word "willing". After all, it was "willingness" in the mind of God that began the plan for Christmas. God was willing to send His Son into the world because he was not willing that man should perish but have everlasting life (2 Peter 3:9). Christ willingly surrendered His life to a cruel, substitutional death on the cross to pay the judicial demands of a Holy Father on a sinful world. As Jesus faced that horror of death He boldly prayed "not my will but thine be done" (Matthew 26:39).

Amazingly enough, it is that very willingness of God, to allow his Son's death to be exchanged for each person's death, that brings meaning to the coming of God's Son. However, people who come to the Father to complete that exchange cannot come with excuses. God's requirements for exchange are in keeping with His own nature of righteousness: "repentance toward God, and faith toward our Lord Jesus Christ." (Acts 20:21). God simply calls men to come to Him with godly sorrow for their sin and a desire to be done with it (this is called repentance), and belief in the death, burial and resurrection of Jesus as payment for sin (this is faith toward our Lord). In coming to God on these terms, Jesus Himself makes this promise: "Verily, verily, I say unto you, He that hears my word, and believes on him that sent me, has everlasting life, and shall not come into condemnation; but is passed from death unto life" (John 5:24).

Now in this "What I really wanted" season, would it not be a wise thing to prioritize all that life is about and exchange your imminent death and judgment from the Holy Father with the everlasting life of the Son? "For the wages of sin [is] death; but the gift of God [is] eternal life through Jesus Christ our Lord" (Romans 6:23).

Personal Notes:

December 28
Galatians 6:1-10

Brethren, if a man is overtaken in any trespass, you who are spiritual restore such a one in a spirit of gentleness, considering yourself lest you also be tempted. Bear one another's burdens, and so fulfil the law of Christ. For if anyone thinks himself to be something, when he is nothing, he deceives himself. But let each one examine his own work, and then he will have rejoicing in himself alone, and not in another. For each one shall bear his own load. Let him who is taught the word share in all good things with him who teaches. Do not be deceived, God is not mocked; for whatever a man sows, that he will also reap. For he who sows to his flesh will of the flesh reap corruption, but he who sows to the Spirit will of the Spirit reap everlasting life. And let us not grow weary while doing good, for in due season we shall reap if we do not lose heart. Therefore, as we have opportunity, let us do good to all, especially to those who are of the household of faith.

Fowl Language

Albert Schweitzer spoke of the lesson of the geese. As a medical missionary he had observed a flock of wild geese settling to rest on a pond, whereupon one of the flock was caught by a crafty gardener who clipped its wings before again releasing it. When the flock attempted to resume their journey, the clipped bird was unable to lift itself into the air. The other geese, observing his struggle, flew about in obvious efforts to encourage him; yet to no avail. Consequently, the entire flock settled back down on the pond and waited until the damaged bird could again fly. The gardener, being rebuked by the loyalty he saw in the geese, watched over them until they were able to resume their long flight.

There are many references in scripture to lessons from God's creation that men should learn. Although the loyalty demonstrated by a flock of geese is not specifically mentioned in scripture, the principle certainly is! Paul, writing to the Galatians said: "Bear ye one another's burdens, and so fulfil the law of Christ" (Galatians 6:2). John wrote: "If anyone has material possessions and sees his brother in need but has no pity on him, how can the love of God be in him? Dear children, let us not love with words or tongue but with actions and in truth" (1 John 3 NIV). James declared: "Religion that

God our Father accepts as pure and faultless is this: to look after orphans and widows in their distress and to keep oneself from being polluted by the world" (James 1:27 NIV).

These apostles and teachers learned well from their Lord and Saviour, Jesus Christ. He himself taught: "Greater love has no-one than this, that he lay down his life for his friends" (John 15 NIV). This principle of loyalty to the acceptance of personal sacrifice was exemplified by Jesus who "being found in appearance as a man, he humbled himself and became obedient to death--even death on a cross" (Philippians 2:8 NIV). This principle of loyalty is the expression of the true disciples of Jesus: "A new command I give you: Love one another. As I have loved you, so you must love one another. By this all men will know that you are my disciples, if you love one another." (John 13 NIV)

The very word for love used in these passages of scripture must be defined as a self-sacrificing loyalty to another. As a new year dawns, and assessment of life's impact is made, one good question that Christians should ask is this: "Is my life marked by self-sacrificing loyalty to others?" Within the relationships of the home, throughout our responsibilities at work, in our service within the church, in our activity within the community, is our life seen as "love spelled L-O-Y-A-L-T-Y?" May the only "fowlness" we allow in our lives be that of modelling the lesson of the geese!

Personal Notes:

December 29
Genesis 4:3-12

And in the process of time it came to pass that Cain brought an offering of the fruit of the ground to the LORD. Abel also brought of the firstborn of his flock and of their fat. And the LORD respected Abel and his offering, but He did not respect Cain and his offering. And Cain was very angry, and his countenance fell. So the LORD said to Cain, "Why are you angry? And why has your countenance fallen? "If you do well, will you not be accepted? And if you do not do well, sin lies at the door. And its desire is for you, but you should rule over it." Now Cain talked with Abel his brother; and it came to pass, when they were in the field, that Cain rose up against Abel his brother and killed him. Then the LORD said to Cain, "Where is Abel your brother?" He said, "I do not know. Am I my brother's keeper?" And He said, "What have you done? The voice of your brother's blood cries out to Me from the ground. "So now you are cursed from the earth, which has opened its mouth to receive your brother's blood from your hand. "When you till the ground, it shall no longer yield its strength to you. A fugitive and a vagabond you shall be on the earth."

My Brother's Keeper

After killing his brother, Cain attempted denial of any guilt. His response to God's inquiry: "Am I my brother's keeper?" marks the essence of human depravity. Man, having denied God, is at the very heart, full of self-interest at the cost of others. Scripture describes man's heart: "The heart is deceitful above all things, and desperately wicked" (Jeremiah 17:9).

One of the beautiful things about trusting in Christ as personal Saviour is the newness this faith affords: "Therefore if any man be in Christ, he is a new creature: old things are passed away; behold, all things are become new" (2 Corinthians 5:17). The new believer, being dwelt within by the Holy Spirit, begins to go through God designed changes: "But the fruit of the Spirit is love, joy, peace, longsuffering, gentleness, goodness, faith, meekness, self-control" (Galatians 5:22-23a).

This newness places God's own, self sacrificing love within. This expresses itself in true care of others: "By this shall all men know that ye are my disciples, if ye have love one to another" (John 13:35). It is to this end that Christians are urged to care for one another: "And we urge you, brothers, warn those who are unruly, encourage the fainthearted, help the weak, be patient with everyone. Make sure that nobody pays back wrong for wrong, but always try to be kind to each other and to everyone else" (1 Thessalonians 5:14-15).

The Christian "law of care" is three fold. Love cares enough to "Admonish the Disorderly." This involves gently correcting those fellow believers who are out of step with God's will by the obvious neglect of spiritual duty, or who are purposefully creating disharmony. Love cares enough to "Encourage the Fainthearted." This involves consoling those fellow believers who are discouraged. This is a ministry of tenderness and compassion to the shaken. Finally, love cares enough to "Support the Weak." Here is a word picture of the strong soldier carrying the wounded comrade.

In his autobiography, Booker T. Washington writes: "The most trying ordeal that I was forced to endure as a slave boy ... was the wearing of a flax shirt... I can scarcely imagine any torture, except for perhaps, the pulling of a tooth, that is equal to that caused by putting on a new flax shirt for the first time. It is almost equal to the feeling that one would experience if he had a dozen or more chestnut burrs, or a hundred small pin-points, in contact with his flesh ... But I had no choice. I had to wear the flax shirt or none ... My brother John, who is several years older than I am, performed one of the most generous acts that I ever heard of one slave relative doing for another. On several occasions when I was being forced to wear a new flax shirt, he generously agreed to put it on in my stead and wear it for several days, till it was "broken in".

God's call is for each believer to be His brother's keeper!

Personal Notes:

December 30

James 1:2-12

My brethren, count it all joy when you fall into various trials, knowing that the testing of your faith produces patience. But let patience have its perfect work, that you may be perfect and complete, lacking nothing. If any of you lacks wisdom, let him ask of God, who gives to all liberally and without reproach, and it will be given to him. But let him ask in faith, with no doubting, for he who doubts is like a wave of the sea driven and tossed by the wind. For let not that man suppose that he will receive anything from the Lord; he is a double-minded man, unstable in all his ways. Let the lowly brother glory in his exaltation, but the rich in his humiliation, because as a flower of the field he will pass away. For no sooner has the sun risen with a burning heat than it withers the grass; its flower falls, and its beautiful appearance perishes. So the rich man also will fade away in his pursuits. Blessed is the man who endures temptation; for when he has been approved, he will receive the crown of life which the Lord has promised to those who love Him.

A Burro of Patience

There is a poster in my office, a prayer that goes like this: "Lord, please give me patience, AND I WANT IT RIGHT NOW!" Humorous as it is, that poster reflects the nature of my own impatience, and reminds me of Paul's exhortation: "And we urge you, brothers, warn those who are idle, encourage the timid, help the weak, be patient with everyone" (1 Thessalonians 5:14 NIV).

The reader of the Epistle to the Thessalonians can imagine the silence that this word of patience invoked when first read among the believers of that city. They had suffered much under the strong arm of those opposed to the gospel of Christ. City leaders had become jealous of Paul's successful ministry. When they failed to locate Paul after many embraced Christ, they took one of the new believers named Jason before the officials and accused him of harbouring traitors. Later, opponents of Christianity from this city traveled to nearby Berea in an effort to destroy the church of Christ there. One can imagine the tendency for the believers, under such persecution and opposition, to become very impatient, yet Paul challenged them to "be patient with all men!"

Paul understood that the true believer in Christ, being indwelt by the Holy Spirit, can do in Christ's power, what man could not do on his own. Not only is the believer called to the law of care, as his brothers keeper, he is also called to the law of patience toward all. Living this out in life is possible as each believer allows the Holy Spirit to produce His love in the life (see Galatians 5:22-23). Scripture reveals patience to be a by-product of God's love: "Love is patient, love is kind... it is not easily angered, it keeps no record of wrongs... It always protects, always trusts, always hopes, always perseveres. Love never fails" (1 Corinthians 13 NIV).

John Killinger retells the following story from "Atlantic Monthly". "A little burro sometimes would be harnessed to a wild steed. Bucking and raging, convulsing like drunken sailors, the two would be turned loose like Laurel and Hardy to proceed out onto the desert range. They could be seen disappearing over the horizon, the great steed dragging that little burro along and throwing him about like a bag of cream puffs."

"They might be gone for days, but eventually they would come back. The little burro would be seen first, leading the submissive steed in tow. Somewhere out there on the rim of the world, that steed would become exhausted from trying to get rid of the burro, and in that moment, the burro would take mastery and become leader."

The trials of Christian experience that provoke impatience are little burros that sent from God to build dependence upon Him. The best God does in the Christian life involves patience. The submissive believer will discover God's love to be the patience of Christ who "was oppressed and afflicted, yet opened not his mouth" (Isaiah 53:7).

Personal Notes:

December 31
Psalm 106:1-12

Praise the LORD! Oh, give thanks to the LORD, for He is good! For His mercy endures forever. Who can utter the mighty acts of the LORD? Who can declare all His praise? Blessed are those who keep justice, And he who does righteousness at all times! Remember me, O LORD, with the favour You have toward Your people; Oh, visit me with Your salvation, That I may see the benefit of Your chosen ones, That I may rejoice in the gladness of Your nation, That I may glory with Your inheritance.

We have sinned with our fathers, We have committed iniquity, We have done wickedly. Our fathers in Egypt did not understand Your wonders; They did not remember the multitude of Your mercies, But rebelled by the sea—the Red Sea. Nevertheless He saved them for His name's sake, That He might make His mighty power known. He rebuked the Red Sea also, and it dried up; So He led them through the depths, As through the wilderness. He saved them from the hand of him who hated them, And redeemed them from the hand of the enemy. The waters covered their enemies; There was not one of them left. Then they believed His words; They sang His praise.

New Year Reflection

Coming to another New Year is like a traveller coming to the pinnacle of a mountain. It is a time to pause and reflect upon the journey past. Before heading into a new valley of yet unknown adventures, the pilgrim looks back over the trodden path and from the mountain vantage point contemplates the experiences of each significant landmark stretched out below. It is a time to ask some self-searching questions.

One of the most important questions to ask is this: "Have I grown in my knowledge of God?" This is not a question about regular church attendance, nor is it about faithful giving. It is not a question about listening to a particular minister or benefiting from a particular church. It is not a question regarding religion, but a question of relationship.

Perhaps the question should be asked with a scriptural perspective: Enoch "walked with God". Have I, this past year? David was "a man after God's own heart" . Does a look back reveal the same of me? Ruth cried to Naomi, "Your God shall be My

God". Have I chosen to make the living God My God this past year? While Martha was cumbered with cares, Mary chose the better path and "sat at Jesus' feet". Have I taken time out from busy schedule to personally sit at Jesus' feet?

If, when looking back over the trodden path of a year gone by, our relationship with the Lord has not grown, then our travels have been in vain; for there is nothing more important in life than knowing the Giver of Life "better every day". This was the apostle Paul's greatest personal desire: "I count all things loss for the excellency of the knowledge of Christ Jesus my Lord" (Philippians 3:8). This was Paul's prayer for the church: "I... cease not to give thanks for you, making mention of you in my prayers; that the God of our Lord Jesus Christ, the Father of glory, may give unto you the spirit of wisdom and revelation in the knowledge of him." (Ephesians 1)

May the words of Charles Spurgeon in the New Year of 1855 cause each reader to reflect on this passing year and focus on this coming year with a purpose to know the Lord. He stated: "The highest science, the loftiest speculation, the mightiest philosophy, which can engage the attention of the child of God, is the name, the nature, the person, the work, the doings, and the existence of the great God whom he calls his Father...There is something exceedingly improving to the mind in a contemplation of the Divinity. It is a subject so vast, that all thoughts are lost in its immensity; so deep, that our pride is drowned on its infinity."

May Christ's prayer impress the importance of this focus on our minds: "And this is life eternal, that they might know thee the only true God, and Jesus Christ, whom thou hast sent." (John 17:3)

Personal Notes:

Made in the USA
Charleston, SC
25 June 2016